John Younger

River Angling for Salmon and Trout

John Younger

River Angling for Salmon and Trout

ISBN/EAN: 9783744791274

Printed in Europe, USA, Canada, Australia, Japan

Cover: Foto ©Lupo / pixelio.de

More available books at **www.hansebooks.com**

RIVER ANGLING.

J Mc Intosh. Photo. Kelso

Eng^d by W Banks & Son. Edin^r

Affectionally yours

John Younger

Published by J. & J. H. Rutherford, Kelso

A manly heart lost this our Border land,

When thine, O Younger, to the grave was borne ;

And friends, even some who never clasped thy hand,

In every valley thy departure mourn ;

For generous hearts are few upon the earth

And genial natures, such as guided thee :

Grave thoughts and sad swept o'er thee, but thy mirth

Out-rode them all—a life-boat on the sea :

And 'mong thy friends how many felt the charm

Of thy keen intellect and racy tongue !

Thy tide of thoughts, thy feelings ever warm,

Portrayed a nature deep, and fresh, and young

Even in thine age ; and long thy name will stand

Respected, honoured, loved, on thine own Border land.

RIVER ANGLING

FOR

SALMON AND TROUT.

BY

JOHN YOUNGER.

WITH A

MEMOIR, AND LIST OF THE TWEED SALMON CASTS.

There are who think these pastimes scarce humane,
Yet in my mind (and not relentless I)
His life is pure that wears no fouler stains.
Armstrong.

KELSO : J. & J. H. RUTHERFURD.
EDINBURGH : WILLIAM BLACKWOOD & SONS.
———
MDCCCLXIV.

PRINTED BY J. AND J. H. RUTHERFURD, KELSO.

ADVERTISEMENT.

WHEN the last Edition of RIVER ANGLING was partly printed (1860), the death of the Author caused it to appear in a less complete state as to arrangement of matter than it would otherwise have done. In the present Edition this has been carefully attended to by the Editor, an experienced Angler; and from this, and the supplementary chapters by him on Creeper Fishing, etc., the Publishers confidently issue the present Volume as a complete work on River Angling for Salmon and Trout.

KELSO, *February* 1864.

CONTENTS.

———◆———

SKETCH OF THE AUTHOR'S LIFE.

If he should not have been successful in any of his intentions, yet there remains this consolation behind—that these, his pursuits, by keeping the body and mind employed, have under Providence, contributed to much health and cheerfulness of spirits—even to old age.—Gilbert White.

WHILE the work now presented to river anglers was passing through the press, a painful incident, and one deeply connected with its matured completion, occurred in the death of the author. A pang of sorrow, such as only the loss of many endearing qualities could occasion, shot through many a heart within miles of his residence, as it was spread from lip to lip that John Younger was dead. On a long summer day, the 19th of June, when the pleasant sights and objects of his " dear native valleys" wore their freshest aspect, John Younger died. For some time previous, his hardy compact frame, that had stood the buffets of a life longer than the common span, shewed signs of decay. There is little doubt that poverty, with its saddening distractions, weighed upon the elasticity of his nature. Physical ailments,

1

of the class that would have been greatly modified by easier circumstances, had begun to drag him back from various literary enterprises, which his attempts at public lectures had marked out. The lithe motion of body and of limb became touched with the proofs of declining strength; yet, his many personal friends never doubted on counting on his familiar presence for years to come. Death, however, came quickly and sternly, and after a brief struggle with a paralytic seizure, John Younger succumbed. In his views of life, and its allotments of trial, he had ever cherished a wish that his end might come under circumstances in which he wouldleave the world without being a tax or trouble to any. The wish was gratified; and the week that saw him looking from the river head-lands of his beautiful Lessudden, saw him also lying in St Boswells' churchyard.

It is trite enough to remark, that John Younger was no common man. His equal has seldom been seen in the class to which he belonged. When it is borne in mind that his education was exceedingly meagre, costing from first to last not more than is now expended on a middle class child in one quarter— that he plodded along in the same groove of occupation and habit all his life long—and had few opportunities of being abroad, and obtaining for his natural acuteness of observation the extended range of objects that is essential to enlarged mental culture, the conviction is forced upon the observer who offers an estimate of him, that, falling in at his proper place he was one of these men of mother wit, original ideas, and marked capacity, who, in Scotland, are represented by Robert Burns, and Hugh Miller, John Leyden, and The Ettrick Shepherd.

As a follower of the somewhat lightly esteemed, but essential avocation of shoemaker, he belongs to the illustrious craft from among whose awls and lasts have come, according to Coleridge (in defiance of the stale Latinism), some patriots of large soul, theologians with pale faces, and hair crisp with study, missionaries of world-embracing christian zeal, critics, and their victims—the builders of the lofty rhyme.

As we find from the autobiography, which during a course of many years he had prepared, "he was the child of honest parents, the youngest of a family of six, was born at Langnewton, in the parish of Ancrum, on the 5th of July, 1785." Langnewton standing on the high banks of the Ale, at that time had pretentions to rank as a Scottish village, from which, by the rural changes, it has passed into a seldom seen, unvisited hamlet. It had the usual

village characteristics, and Younger commenced the
school of observation on what he saw and heard in
it. There was the now obsolete weaver of "customer
wark," the never to be obsolete blacksmith, with his
nightly band of quidnuncs, such as Burns saw when
a boy—the ploughman, the day labourer, the poacher,
the hand-spinning matron, the dominie, and the
way-faring "Daft Jock." Towards it, as the place
of his nativity, and of the earliest and most varied
recollections of his life, his heart always yearned.
In the Ale he caught his first trout, and under an
ash tree, in a corner of the churchyard of the village,
was his mother's grave.

Sixty years ago Scotland was a poor country. She
had been fighting during all her history out of a
cold soil, a wet climate, and a certain sourness or
grim earnestness of character, acquired by long contact with hard times—social, civil, religious and
agrarian—when the black famine years, that saw
out the old century and ushered the new one in,
made clean teeth throughout the land. It may well
be imagined what were the sharp household straits
that children with empty stomachs had to struggle
through. The quarter loaf rose to close on two shillings. Wheat stood at one hundred and twenty-five
shillings a quarter. Parliament, by statute, enforced

economy in the use of bread, prohibiting its consumption until it had been baked for twenty-four hours. The slip of an urchin did not even enjoy the licence of cow-herding. To make ends meet in his father's struggles, he was early encased in a sheep-skin apron, and made to jerk out his elbows in drawing rosined thread. A conscript seized upon the village green, he possessed native instincts that soon sharpened into faculties, and he sought companionship with members of animated nature. The boy became an adept in the knowledge of birds and beasts; and hawks, blear-eyed owls, and flippant jack daws, squatted around him. Bird cages blocked up the light of day, and the shoemaker's shop, the lounge of village gossipers, was vocal with the contending songs of whole coveys of linnets and canaries. John often wondered how his honest father tolerated such an uproar. Out of doors he early picked up a knowledge of the habits and kinds of birds. The slightest twit in a hedge or wood, would tell its name; and he did not require the old poacher, who sat smoking on the settle of the yellow-ochred cottage door, to tell him the destination, on the minnowy stream, of the great flaunting heron which sailed high over the village chimney tops. The best angler to this day is he who knows most about the habitat of the finny

tribe ; and the shoemaker lad, with his quick per-
ceptions, learnt how to catch trout almost at his will.
He would cut his hazel* wand from the young wood,
and though the trouts might be shy to the nicest turn
out of rod and tackle, he would come home with the
bunching strap of silvery spoils, till all the village
lads looked amazed.   This was the fashion in which
the author of the present work furnished the proof
of his early attainments in the gentle art.

There needed to be no readier sign of the natural
cleverness of the prentice shoemaker than his water-
side craft.   In his own words, " he flew to the Ale
water and fished for trout as much for his dinner as
for amusement."   In the dear years a dinner pur-
veyed with so little labour was not to be despised,
for these were dreadful times.   They have served all
the men who fasted in the pinches of the hungry
epoch with a tale of such distress as has not died
out till this day.   How often have readers of this
notice heard old men narrate the dismal story of
meal at seven shillings the stone !   Flodden itself has
hardly sent down to after times so sad a *sough* as

Hazel seems to be a kind of wood that anglers instinctively draw
to ; anglers at least who cannot pay for shop-made rods.   In Walton's
time it was the favourite wood, and James Baillie, accounted by
several authors and many anglers the best fly-fisher of the present
day, angles daily with a two-piece hazel rod cut from the wood-bank,
and angled with as cut.—[EDR.]

have those dear years! We find few written records of them too. They were too early for our best working-class autobiographers, Hugh Miller and Somerville. When John Younger's autobiography is given to the world we will have the right idea how the poorer families fared. His share in it was not small, for he had nearly perished from the long want of sufficient sustenance. He has described himself as the member of the family, who, with his natural shiftiness, was selected to seek credit at the corn mills in the neighbourhood where meal was sold. When he had procured a supply he set off at full speed (for he knew the household was at the starving point), running over the dreary fields with the pock under his arm. Temptation would assail him, and he would untwist the neck of the bag, and gulp down with hungry hurry the dry meal, and then, lest he should be tempted again, he would twirl up the neck beyond ready reach, and run with additional speed. What a picture of the times is here presented! The Scottish people may well cherish the memory of the period with pride, for they endured the trial nobly. The sensitiveness as to accepting parochial relief even survived the crisis. John Younger's account may enable even statesmen to compare the different ways in which the Scotch and the

Irish have borne up against the calamities of famine.

John Younger was a manly-hearted boy, and strove to utter no murmur in his hard pressed father's hearing. He bore up against despondency, and like Bunyan, he even owned to a bit of monologue; for one day, while staring into a pool of water, he fancied his shadow accosted him by saying, "keep up yer heart Jock Younger, keep up yer heart ma man Jock." Jock took the hint, and heaven sent brighter days.

John's first contact with literature deserves to be noted. He had read Jack the Giant Killer, and scarcly dreamed of anything higher than the great nursery epic. A blacksmith in advance of his time repeated a portion of "Doctor Hornbook," mentioning the name of Burns, who was then only a few years dead. The slenderly versed shoemaker asked " whae was Burns?"—"Burns, man (was the rejoinder), have ye never heard of Burns the poet, who beats Allan Ramsay, and the whole lot of Scotch poets to sticks!" John heard the bookish Burnewin with melancholy curiosity, and sighed at the idea, of exclusion from such poetic wealth. But St Boswells' fair came, and he sallied up the thronged alleys between the krames with sixpence in his pocket, and grasped the prize of his heart, a sewed copy of the said "Burns' Poems." Home he went, for the fair had no further charms for him. Into the heart of a blackberry bush, that flourished with a kind of arbour shape in his father's garden, he tumbled, and, with a bright disdain, left the showman-spoutings, the busy hum, the gaudy, touting, holiday enticements, to those who cared for them.

The village of Bowden was not far off. A line from Clapperton, an old Scotch poet, " at Bowden, on black Monanday," shews that the village had received poetic mention. In addition to being the birth place of Thomas Aird, the imperfect fulfiller of great poetic promise, it takes credit for fostering the nativity of Andrew Scott, the author of the quaint but classic piece of dialogue rhythm " Symon and Janet," beginning,

> Surroundit wi' bent, an' wi' heather,
> 　Where muircocks an' plivers are rife,
> For mony lang towmond thegether,
> 　There lived an auld man an' his wife.

To Andrew, John made up and was received with kindliness. In return, John rendered homage as to genius, and a friendship was formed, lasting till the old barnman flung down the flail never to uplift it.

The era of the false alarm, originating in the juncture of Buonaparte's threatened invasion, was a period of vivid sensations to the subject of our notice, as it was to most at that time. He was strutting on the top of his teens, and shouldered a firelock as a member of the Militia Corps. This he did with a perfect consciousness expressed all through life, that fighting was the most abject of all human occupations. The trade of soldiering was abhorrent to his moral sense and the habits of his mind ; and no member of the peace society could have more scrupulously examined the motives under which he appeared as a defender of his country. In one of his opinions on the subject, afterwards recorded, he says, " it is very distressing for the human mind to contemplate the dire movement of congregated masses of flesh and blood, dragged out in the train of hellish ambition for the most horrible purposes, following individuals who shew themselves so utterly unworthy of even personal existence." On the night on which the beacons were lighted, the 31st January, 1804, when the heart of the nation heaved in one fiery swell of patriotic feeling, John marched to the place of rendezvous, ten miles distant, and tore his trousers in scaling the palisades of Kelso bridge toll-house. The grotesque features of his night's adventures, full many a time and oft he was wont to bring up at the annual convivial meeting, held at St Boswells to this day, to commemorate the historic event, and the story never grew tiresome in the telling.

At twenty-five, John had settled in life, had a wife, Agnes Riddle by name, and a house of his own, shoemaking his trade, and St Boswells or Lessudden his residence for life. In a notice of a man who, spent his days in following one of the most plebeian of occupations, it is difficult to find individual incidents to make out the track of his existence. His original thinking powers soon marked him off as one who could not be invisible in the dead inertness of rural life. On the north side of the village was a picture of silvan and river scenery, in the winding of the peerless Tweed, such as might have haunted any man possessing less idealism than John, with the pleasure which nature in her diviner glimpses yields. There was Dryburgh, rearing its time-stricken gables among the trees ; but strange to say such an object excited no pleasure in John. These haunts of monks and their worn out superstitions he despised, as having formed part of the imposture which had retarded freedom of ideas and common sense among men. He had more true delight in watching the motions of the water ousel skipping and coquetting on the river shallows, or in listening to the snatch of the red-breast's pleasant or plaintive carol on the apple tree, than in the survey of all the abbeys of Domesday book. " The monks (with him) were dead and buried, and let them lie, without bringing them on the stage of life, where they had done so little to deserve mankind's respect." Curious to say he did not care at all for the writings of Sir Walter Scott. With some who knew him little, this may be set down to an absence of true imaginative culture, but the fact was, it arose out of a quaint peculiarity of mind. He looked on the Waverley literature as " old piper stories," " dwarf and witch tales," and monstrous caricatures, of Scottish manners. He never threw himself in Scott's way, though living in the same locality. When he sauntered to the top of the village cliff to look riverward, and sniff the western breeze, the object in the landscape which the resting place of the minstrel formed, would catch his eye and yet excite no passing sigh.

The following work will have suggested that fishing was one of his greatest sources of recreation. In the course of years it passed from recreation almost to regular occupation. The Tweed, the stately stream, in its scenic associations and bright remembrances of sport, and friends, and merry hours, became the silver bond that knitted all his sympathies to the locality of St Boswells. The kind of Austrian rigour with which angling privilege on the river is now protected had then no existence. There is not a shadow of a doubt that the Tweed was then far more the poor man's river than it is now. Things stood on an easier footing between laird and commoner. John Haliburton, on his perch of Craig-o'er, rented the Merton water at fifteen pounds a-year, with a cow's grass, and often as he passed his friend, the shoemaker's door, he called out a kindly invitation for him to come down and get a cast. Younger's great natural powers of observation, conjoined with a wary watchfulness of fish, and steady practice at the rod, united in making him a proficient in the art. His reputation increased as his friendships extended, and from far and near, his fishing knowledge and company were courted. Apart altogether from his literary turn and tendency to blacken paper, he was marked off as a man of note, and hailed as a " Tweedside Gnostic." The shoemaker's shop was a house of call for all the Waltonian brotherhood : dukes, lords, Galashiels weavers, escaped Parliament men, squires, cotton lords, and the whole medley whose boot heels ever

crunched the pebbly shore of the glorious river or
its tributaries, came at times to hear John Younger
discourse on the theme, which, ahead of rivals, he
had so well mastered.   And what a *crack* was his !
And how meagre and few the souls for whom it
possessed no relish.   He could tell the waggle of the
wand that could most deftly throw the line, and the
bits of wood that, pieced together, made up the best
style of rod.   Rods he could manufacture on the
shrewdest principle of effect.   Fishing tackle and
hooks he knew by intuition; for how a salmon
viewed things as he lay in his watery haunt was
part of the fishing art.   The occupation of shoemaker
made fishing boots ready to his hand, and he
came to be noted for his skill in the fabrication of
these gentlemanly appurtenances of the pursuit :
but it is unnecessary to dwell with any minuteness
on this branch of his many acquirements, as the
following essay discloses all the proofs of a most extensive knowledge of the subject.

Out of all the wide variety of friendly contacts,
it may be assumed that John Younger had many
opportunities of increasing his knowledge of the
ideas current in the world beyond the sphere in
which he had to make his bread.   The late Sir
Robert Peel, in one of his speeches, said he had

studied the wants of the nation by contact with the highest personages of the realm, and had conversed with the Highland shepherd on the hills, and heard him tell his artless views of human life ; and many a member of the governing class, or of the " upper ten thousand," would discuss public affairs in perfect equality with the obscure shoemaker, and perhaps gather conviction on some point which he had failed to elicit amid the contentions of party and the perplexities of unconscious prejudice. On one occasion when the Hon. J. E. Elliot was visiting his constituency, being Member for Roxburgh-shire, he happened to call in a friendly way upon his friend the shoemaker, who, talking of political affairs, remarked, that he never had enjoyed an opportunity of seeing Lord John Russell ; and that with his recollections of public men it would be a pleasure to him just to shake hands with a politician whose personal integrity men of all shades of opinion respect. No sooner said than done. The worthy member got John Younger crushed into the carriage beside him, and whirled him off to Minto House, where Lord John Russell happened to be on a visit ; and there and then he left the two to a conversation, such as produced a lively impression of pleasure upon both parties.

We are aware that John Younger came to be viewed with some jealousy, as a man who held extreme political opinions. With his outspoken disposition, and forcible powers of expression, he could hardly escape such an imputation. In this respect we think he was misjudged. He was a poor man, and naturally took the side that poor men take when questions affecting popular privileges are under discussion; but he was remarkably free from all political crotchets. When the chartist movement was at its formidable stage he was invited to take part in it, but declined, seeing no good results to follow, and imputing to it not a few bad ones at the period. He has recorded the following remark on political discussion : "The man who will tell me that because I am a poor man, I have no business with the government of my country, I must despise as something worse than a simple idiot." He has the following just remarks on public affairs, and the principle by which they should be conducted. "A continual stirring, in what are called state contentions, is kept up by parties for public offices, in idea of honour or profit, or both; but these are comparatively like winds and storms to the balance of the general atmosphere, partial and trivial in their effects, compared with the spirit of the exclusive principle,

which is ever generative of those heartburnings
which excite to political volcanoes, eruptions, and
earthquakes." The Reform Bill he hailed as a great
and just measure, constituting " an inestimable
general privilege," which " would exercise a whole-
some influence over the tergiversations, and abuses
of public trust by the governing few."

On the corn laws, the repeal of which has done
more to *sweeten the breath*, as Dr Chalmers phrased it,
of British society than any measure in living memory,
John Younger vented his hottest ire ; their evils he
summed in few words—they hood-winked the far-
mer, and raised to the poor man the price of bread.
He heaped on these laws his bitterest scorn, and
threw off various Corn Law Rhymes to fan the
flame which their prolongation was exciting. Some
of these found their way to Ebenezer Elliott, the
Corn Law Rhymer of Sheffield, who, in a letter of
acknowledgment, asked why their author wasted his
strength in verse when he possessed so much natural
energy as a prose writer. Elliott's letter was accompanied by a gift of a complete edition of his
works, of which John was exceedingly proud.

Twelve years, however, before the corn laws closed
their account of social and civil mischief, John
Younger had registered himself an author. In 1834

2

he gave to the world a small publication, entitled
" Thoughts as they Rise," a poem in Byronic measure. It was an attempt at a poem, constructed
" without an imaginary hero, romanting through its
cantos." Whether owing to the plot wanting thus
confessedly the part of Hamlet, or to the disrelish
on the part of the public, for moralizations by a
shoemaker on human affairs, the work fell still-born
from the press, and further cantos, which were
threatened, John kept to himself.

The poem is, however, a remarkable production
for a working man, if we consider the command over
the English language, the easiness of versification,
the occasional force and beauty of the sentiments
which it betrays.

At random we make an extract:

" And so I envy none their lands and dower,
   Nor all that they can claim below the skies,
Yet can't resist the wish I had the power,
   To wipe the tear from modest mourning eyes.
How blest to deck the lowly humble bower
   With winter fire, and summer sunshine joys,
Change many a sigh of want into a song,
And cause the stream of life flow clear along.
    *   *   *   *

Or this picture of rural zest:

" O, how I love the moorland scene of spring
   Beneath the smile of morning's ruddy glow,
The whirr of heath-cock, and the curving swing
   Of snipe high booming o'er the marshy flow—
The fond solicitude of flapping wing,

To lead the wanderer from the nest below;
I love the *swuff* of every out-field feather—
By wood or stream, or 'mid the purple heather."

With the bulk of men engaged in manual occupations, writing is irksome and slow work; the fingers are stiff, and the connexion between brain and pen-holding is an awkward task. John Younger was an exception to all this. He would beat his lapstone and draw his thread all day, and betake himself for relief to letter writing. His invariable plan was to make his knees his writing desk, and in this uninviting attitude the great bulk of his MS. was produced; not scrawled and blotched, but presented in a small clear elegant penmanship, which in the case of a self-taught workman is rarely met with. With friends at a distance, men who had left St Boswells for the broader field of adventure and pursuit which it could not supply, or friends of a chance intimacy, he maintained an extensive correspondence, making his epistles so much the record of his careful thinking that he took copies of them. In this way an immense quantity of manuscript accumulated in the course of years, significant of the ceaseless mental activity which characterised him. At his death there were more than seven hundred copies of letters which he had addressed to friends. Many of these had been written to men of literary eminence or public distinction, giving his views of the opinions associated with their names. This collection he cherished as the treasure of his mental history. Sometimes when leaving home he used to warn his family that if the house took fire in his absence, next to saving themselves they should save these writings. Composition coming so readily to him, and friends often hinting the propriety of the step, he betook himself, after the period of middle life, to prepare an autobiography, a species of personsal narrative always interesting, no matter what may have been the limited sphere of existence of the writer. The work in his hands grew from less to great, so that some years before his death it amounted to the contents of two goodly volumes.

It contains much racy description of local occurrences and manifestations of village character, beginning with life at Langnewton, and following on in narration of the fate, fortunes, and families of his acquaintance. The publication of the work will, we trust, be not long deferred ; and we venture to describe it such as will form a genuine accession to autobiographic literature.

Shoemaking was but a poor trade to a man struggling with a family, and pulled at by needy friends ; and it was to be regretted that so much literary industry, as he displayed, brought such slight rewards. On several occasions he received an acknowledgment for articles connected with angling or natural history. In 1840 he appeared as the author of the Essay on angling, of which the present work is a re-written edition. He often lamented that he could not bring the knowledge he possessed on many subjects to more account. The year 1847 brought an opportunity by which he could measure his capacity and literary grasp with the men of his class. John Henderson, Esq. of Park, a gentleman distinguished for his zeal in every good cause, by way of directing public opinion to the better observance of the Sabbath, proposed three prizes for the best Essays on the " Temporal advantages of the Sabbath to the labouring classes." John Younger's eye fastened on the public announcement. " The hour and the man" had come together, and he resolved to try his hand in the competition. More than a year passed away, when the intimation was exultingly speeded over the south of Scotland that John Younger had obtained the second prize. A thrill of pleasure cheered Tweedside as the good news was repeated from mouth to mouth, and John became the theme of applauding tongues in every circle. To London he must go to receive the prize of £15 from the Earl

of Shaftesbury in Exeter Hall.   He was whirled out
of Lessudden one afternoon, and the following day
saw him in London lionized amid the plaudits of
multitudes.   It was the triumph which ambition
could have envied, to have seen the north country
shoemaker, with the guileless unpretending presence
standing up to receive the well-won reward.   This
was the greatest event in John Younger's life, and
he ever afterwards referred to it as something, in its
public and exciting accompaniments, far beyond the
possibilities that fate had allotted to his career.

To mark the gratification which was experienced
in the district, by this recognition of his abilities, he
was entertained at a public dinner, in St Boswells
Inn, by a highly respectable gathering, and presented
with a purse of sovereigns.

Upon the solid merits of the " Light of the Week,"
the title of the essay, we need not occupy much
space in remarking.   We question if the author ever
held the pen with a freer or more vigorous style.
The composition is admirable throughout, distinguished by sententious force, picturesque illustrations,
and a vivid logical treatment of the subject, such as
the pulpit or divinity of a heavier texture might
envy.

Shortly after the event, a vacancy having occurred

in the village post office, the appointment was, on
the recommendation of the Hon. J. E. Elliot, at
that time member for the county, conferred upon
John, in the belief that his advancing years would
find an easier living than in toiling at his old trade.
The result, however, proved different from what was
expected. The rigid exactitude of rule, the perplexing net work of forms and business routine, were
more than one accustomed to the simple machinery
of making shoes could overtake, and when the life
was nearly vexed out of him, in January 1856 John
threw up the appointment in disgust. To the present writer and a friend, who called shortly after, he
said he felt himself, when postmaster, like a caged
squirrel running over its never-ending wheel, but
that when he was free he felt himself just like the
squirrel on the top of a tree, " ready to jump
wherever he liked."

The celebration of the Burns' centenary, in 1859,
stimulated John to bring out a lecture on the genius
and character of the national bard. He had a fancy
that he could treat the subject in a way of his own
believing that many traits and perplexing points in
Burns' history had been misunderstood, and that
purely literary men had not been grounded as he
had been in the experience of a social condition,

similar to that from which Burns started, to take the natural and plain, common-sense view of the poet's case. At the very period that old William Burnes* was breaking his heart, and working the flesh off his bones with vexation on the "seven poor acres of nursery ground," near to Alloway Kirk, John Younger's father was making a hard fight to get ends to meet by cobbling shoes and renting a fourteen acre farm on the Langnewton barony. Old Younger had "to thole a factor's snash," like him of Doonside, and the son remembered that the crisis of the household arrived when the cow was distrained for rent.

Like Burns, John Younger, from infancy, had cherished a deep and earnest sympathy with nature. He had all his days loved the country, and never had been a denizen of city or town. The woods, the green fields, the dingles and dells, and shady coverts of the river side, the red-breast perking among the berry bushes of the cottager's garden on a grave autumn day, the blackbird or throstle piping in the budding beech, the great crow armies blackening the fields, or drifting up into mid air with many-throated clangour, and scattering themselves away in the endless fields of sky, the fresh, newly furrowed land,

* Robert Burns spelled his name differently from his father.—[EDR.]

with the white pick-maw sailing about the sober
ploughman's team-gang, the sights and sounds that
had their being ere man betook himself to build
cities and live in masses, were the educating in-
fluences that had made John Younger what he came
to be, and which inspired him with an ambition to
interpret in plain story the life of Robert Burns.
And common consent, though candid enough to
admit that some of his conclusions might be open to
objection, confessed that John Younger was in a large
degree successful in what he had undertaken. His
critical estimate of Burns had a rough matter-of-
fact quality about it. He did not sail in the clouds
in flights of eloquence, or discourse in grand allegori-
cal tropes like Carlyle. With a pooh, pooh, and a
humph of contempt, he ridiculed the so-called romance, " The glory and the joy," with which
imaginative writers had surrounded the bard's existence. Very much romance indeed, he thought,
there was about the greatest man in a nation lying
in a stable loft, and spending his pain-racked mid-
nights amid the perfumes of such an abode, listening to the nags below stirring, stamping, or riving
at the *fusionless* bog hay! He considered that Burns
was too much the companion of every day suffering
to sustain any such picture as Wordsworth had

drawn, and thought that he drove his plough to another tune, that of dour, determined, conquering toil,
tugging at his awkward nags amid the birns and
bumping boulders of a farm which never could yield
meat or clothes, or household peace to the poor tenant.
He thought if ever Burns played a servile part it was
in dedicating his poems to the Caledonian Hunt.
What did such a pack care about poems! They
were a bye word in Scotland at the very time, for a
story had gone abroad that they had hunted a bitch
fox over several miles of country, and at the death
found the poor animal had carried one of its pups all
the way in its mouth. It was a treat to see the un-
affected *bonhomie* of the "old man eloquent," elevated
on the lecture bench, to talk of Burns. He had the
key of a sympathetic fellow-feeling to all the phases
of Burns' life. No one who listened, but admitted
that a shrewder, more instinctive apprehension of
that life, had seldom been produced. When he came
to offer selections of the favourite poems, his warm
loving admiration of the verses knew no bounds.
"Here awa, there awa, wandering Willie," he designated the tenderest and most beautiful love song
which ever came from the lips of man; and as his
voice repeated several of the stanzas, the tributary
tears of emotion coursed down his cheeks. The lec-

ture was delivered in most of the towns and villages in the Border district, and the proceeds were sufficiently respectable to promise, by his extending his tour, what would be a nest egg for the wants of his advancing years. A number of his Border friends resident in Glasgow invited him to the western metropolis to deliver the lecture there. He was able to accomplish the visit, but with unfavourable results to himself. Exposure to extremely severe weather during his movements, brought on an attack of rheumatism, which prostrated and confined him to his lodgings for several weeks. The attendant expense of this misfortune melted away most of his gains, and he reached Lessudden as poor as ever.

During the long and severe winter of 1859-60 he was seldom seen abroad, and did not regain much strength. Generally cheerful and unrepining, he began to confess himself as growing old, and less able for active work at his ordinary trade. In conversation on some of his favourite topics, he regretted he had accomplished so small a portion of what he felt was within his reach. He had a fancy he could prepare several papers on some of the social changes which had come under his observation—furnishing sketches of the rural improvements and altering condition of the population, and cognate subjects. Work of this description he was well able to perform, and he was urged by his friends to over-take it. Daily bread, however, was still with him to be reached by working with the leather apron about him, and he continued to make or cobble shoes, to the extent which his health permitted. For several months he had been less before the public eye, and when the stroke which separated him from all earthly friendships occurred, a painful surprise was created. As we have stated in the opening of this notice, his end came quickly. He had been apparently in nearly his usual health and spirits, and had been persuing his favourite story from the German, " The Journal of a Poor Vicar"— a narrative which he almost knew by heart—when illness, disclosing a hopeless paralytic seizure ensued, and before another day was gone John Younger was dead.

That John Younger was a recognized celebrity was seen in the many genial tributes to his character and attainments which instantly appeared in the Edinburgh and local press—several of them eloquent and lengthy. In the *Scotsman's* article he was designated as " one of the most remarkable men of the population of the south of Scotland ; whether as a genial writer of prose or verse, or a man of high conversational powers, and clear common sense, the shoemaker of St Boswells had few or no rivals in the south—in his death leaving behind him no enemies, and the memory of a guileless, unblameable, honest life."

The *Caledonian Mercury* had a similar kindly notice. Younger's friend for many years, eminent as a scholar and linguist, William Brockie of the *Sunderland Times*, gave a sketch of his character, summing the leading features of his career, thus—"Of poor, but honest and respectable parentage, he continued poor, but honest and respectable; his whole life a hard struggle against poverty, owing in a great measure to unfortunate family and business connections. Happy in wedded life, he was for many years a widower—his children grown up and settled. Nature made him a poet, a philosopher, and a nobleman; society made him a cobbler of shoes (a good one), a postmaster (indifferent), and a mortgaged feuar of Lessudden."

In the village in which he had spent the greater portion of his more than three score years and ten, the death of its most notable man was felt with the pang which friendship feels when its circle is suddenly narrowed. John Younger dead ! he who gave a character to the little town, and who brought many a visitor to it; who always evoked the play of

human nature's kindlier moods.   John was not
adjudged as without faults.   In some of the pursuits
of life he was not a successful man, and perhaps in
a world in which the material measure is apt to be
applied, a short-coming of success is not viewed as
without blame.   He was deficient in practical talent.
Industrious and second to none as a maker of shoes, he
never acquired the art which could carry him beyond
the rank of a small country tradesman.   At times
in his career he had his foot beyond the threshold
of difficulties, when some business or domestic con-
tingency would drag him back, and he was the same
poor man.   It spoke much to the general tone of
his character that even those who might have occasion, by business transactions, to sit in judgment on
him, always stopped short of a harsh conclusion, and
finished with an expression of sympathy or kind
regard.   The warm and respectful feeling shewn
towards him by every one, avouched his possession
of qualities of head and heart honourably combined.
In the village all felt his departure.   The boys and
girls who would not disturb the bird's nest in his
garden, nor furtively abstract the flushing fruit of
his plum tree, will cherish his memory.   The old
inhabitant who had plodded on life's journey, and
had often stepped in to compare notes on public and

local matters, missed the social crack and sneeshin mull. The fascination that was wont to draw delighted listeners, and which stirred so many a bright conversation, and shook out so many a bright idea, which grappled with the dialectics of ever so varied subjects of human enquiry, had disappeared. The end of the pleasant village, with its garden intersections and quaint bye lanes, its crumbling bluff of river wall, and commanding outlook on the umbrageous pomp of wood and stream, had "lost its wierdest and its wariest eye."

> One morn we missed him on the accustomed hill,
>   Along the heath, and near his favourite tree,—
> Another came, nor yet beside the rill,
>   Nor up the lawn, nor at the wood was he.

In personal appearance John Younger had always a hale hardy look. Possessing a frame compactly knit, of moderate height, of an erect open bearing, he wore into years without shewing many traces of age. When a young man he was distinguished by his agility and skill in athletic and manly sport, and he excelled as a pedestrian. The faithful etching prefixed to the volume gives the man in his facial expression as he is remembered by all his friends. There was a guileless, frank kindliness of manner about him, which carried in it the freemasonry of warm fellow-feeling, and placed him at his ease with all with whom he came in contact.

We have in the preceding pages attempted to introduce the reader to a familiar conception of the man as he appeared in his own walk of life, from an impression that the naked publication of the work on angling would have been meagre without some light being thrown upon the character and occupations of its author. We might have enumerated some of the subjects which he illustrated by his descriptive pen ; many of them were fugitive sketches, but in good hands, they would bear a reappearance in a volume of selections. His poetical effusions, always marked by merit, were more a proof of his varied ability than of any strong natural bias to the cultivation of the muse. In summing a notice of his life, it may not be out of place to present a specimen of his success in this department of literary craft. The first piece was written in 1837, and abounds in the home feeling which marked his domestic history. The second breathes a spirit of the tenderest conjugal love, and as a memorial of their married life, is as creditable as it is delicately expressed. John was in the fullest sense a domestic man, a kind and indulgent father, and a faithful husband. For the partner of his life he cherished the affection of his youth. When prostrate with illness during his Glasgow visit, he wrote to his friends at Lessudden, that if he died they were to bring his body to St Boswells churchyard, and lay it beside his Nannie. The sad duty alluded to in the closing stanza fell to be performed by John, his wife's death having preceded his own by several years.

There may be sweeter spots afar
   That I have never seen,
And lofty towers and rivers clear
   With flowery vales between :
And fairer faces too may grace
   The garden and the hall :
But there's a place, and there's a face
   That's dearest of them all.

And O ! our cradle spot of earth—
   Where light first took our e'e,
And mother's love our infant heart—
   Where'er that spot may be :
Tho' it were even slavery's soil
   And we got free to rove,
Yet wander how or where we will,
   'Twill claim our latest love.

The swallow dreams on Afric's shore
   of Scotia's summer pride ;
And plumes her wing, and knows her hour
   To hasten to Tweedside.
The cliff or skaur she kens afar,
   And towering ruins grey,
Where she was nursed—in Dryburgh's bower,
   The lap of flowery May.

The salmon gray of Tweed or Spey,
   Returning from the sea,
Seeks to its native river stream,
   Whichever stream it be.
Even spirits 'mong celestial orbs,
   In glory roaming free,
May own to earth, their first abode,
   A soul-felt sympathy.

And there is yet anither bield
   That ne'er can be forgot—
Tho' in his age from thence expelled—
   My Nannie's father's cot.
In memory's light, like glow-worm gleams,
   My fancy yet recalls
Love's youngest hopes, and downy dreams
   Still nestling round its walls.

MY NANNIE.

Its now full twa an' forty year,
   Since nestling in wi' Nannie;
As weel my part, I held her dear,
   Sae faithfu', young, an' bonnie.
Her tocher was a trifle sma',
   A hard-earned weel-saved pennie;
But o' tocher could I think ava,
   When in my arms my Nannie.

Nae artfu' wiles, plied e'er sae fain,
   Could move the mind o' Nannie;
Had courtiers wooed 'twould been in vain,
   Her heart was held by Johnnie.
Of cares we've had our world's share,
   Through stormy days and sunny;
My part has been the less to bear,
   I've had sic help o' Nannie.

A welding heat o' strong young love
  Will last through winters many;
The frosts of years but tend to prove
  The links that bind to Nannie.
Though teeth are fled, and locks grown gray,
  She's yet sae kind and cannie—
Love that outlasts young life's hey-day
  Is the love I bear my Nannie.

'Mid a' the thoughts that trouble me,
  The saddest thought of ony
Is wha may close the other's e'e—
  May it be me or Nannie?
The ane that's left may sairly feel,
  Amid a world uncanny;
I'd rather brave auld age mysel'
  Than lanely leave my Nannie.

REMARKS PRELIMINARY.

It seems to have been an early practice with anglers, which is yet much followed in books written on the Art of Angling, to face up the subject with pretensions of its being an amusement above all others conducive to religious contemplation. This is silly, either as a notion or a pretence ; and on the other hand it is equally pitiful to read the frivolous sarcasms by which this pursuit is in turn assailed.

Dr Johnson and Lord Byron, these famed fondlings of their age, have said some smart things to render angling ridiculous as a pastime. Having acquired no taste for it themselves, they wished to make believe that they stigmatized it from a moral sentiment ; and this, not so much perhaps from an inclination to

> " Compound for sins they were inclined to
> By damning those they had no mind to,"

as from an opposition to the whimsicalities of early writers on the subject ; such as old Isaac Walton,

and the religious sportswoman of 1496, Dame
Juliana Barnes, who mixed up their descantations
with pretences of its being favourable to holy medi-
tations, from the rural quietude of the pursuit.
This must have been alleged by these early anglers
and writers through a sort of mental defence against
a superstitious suspicion, that it was not perhaps
the most christian way of spending the sweet summer days of a brief probationary term of an eternal
existence. Hence the struggle to the present hour
of a hundred-and-nine scribblers on the subject to
maintain a point, of the propriety of which they
are by no means thoroughly convinced : only, finding the pastime a kind of exercise agreeable to their
propensities—like that of cats to hunt mice, and lords
foxes—they make a specious pretence of considering
its gratification, not only as no sin, but rather in
the light of a duty. Now the truth lies in this as
in many disputed points, midway between the two
extremes. No one who inclines to go a-fishing can
reasonably suppose the pursuit any way very particular in point of morality—let him allege what he
may, we believe that the angler foregoes such con-
siderations. We view the matter simply in this
way, that every man is so much of a boy (which may
often be the best part of his character) that he goes

out a-fishing because he had got into an early habit
of so going, and finds amusement in it preferable
to walking, or even to riding, should he be master of a horse ; or else he pursues it, fain to find
recreation in that in which he perceives his neigh-
bour so well pleased, just as he would go a-quoit-
ing, a-cricketing, or a-curling. To talk of following
it on a principle of love or admiration of field
scenery, the wood-skirted grandeur of cliff or
stream, is surely either a pretence or an illusion
of his own mind ; because every staunch angler
may be said to leave his admiration of the
picturesque, the beautiful, and romantic in nature,
as something to be particularly kept in mind, re-
turned to and enjoyed " at a more convenient
season"—as governor Felix did his taste for the most
sublime doctrines of Christianity. I have felt that
I could admire the beautiful in landscape as much
as my neighbours, perhaps any of them, yet never
could find either taste or time for the disposition of
sentiment while sallying out on a fishing excursion ;
and however romantically beautiful the branch over-
hung its shadow in the water, I no sooner hanked
my hooks on it than, if within reach, crash down it
came, whilst a wish hurried over my mind that all
river-skirting trees were removed. I would hardly

except the bordering willows of Dryburgh, or those skirting the rivers of Babylon, where the Israelites hung their harps in the days of their captivity.

By no poetical feeling whatever should the free swing of line be ever interrupted. Let sketchers put imaginary trees in their landscapes as they please, yet such are ever the true angler's real feelings, disguise them as he may : KEEP TREE, ROCK, AND IVY FULL LINE-SWING FROM THE MARGIN OF LAKE AND STREAM. One truth is worth fifty of these fishing authors' sickly *preachments.* If our tractates on the subject should never sell, let us not heap disgrace on our own poor head by feigning sanctity we never feel. Such would be worse than prevalent superstition or common hypocrisy. I can see no more sentimentality in angling for fish than in the rural sports of Fox or Otter hunting.* The excitement is kept up by the solicitude of success, and this the same in fishing for reputation in the sport, as in fishing for a dinner ; the true angler being always intent in the pursuit, however passive he may appear.

The fertility of Isaac's imagination, and the ingenuity of his mind, would have made him to excel

---

* There is at least a charm, a romance, felt in the prospect or the remembrance of angling which almost every one feels, and which John himself must have felt hundreds of times.—[EDR.]

in whatever his hand might have found to do. A
mind too versatile to have been confined within the
critical rules of any age or art had excited him to
write out his mixed thoughts, feelings, conceits,
songs, and sermons, on all favourite subjects, just as
they occurred to his fancy—hence all are found
pouched up together like his fish baits. Had he
not fallen madly fond of angling pursuits, I have no
doubt but he might have been one of the greatest
devotees of his superstitious age. Or had he turned
to " the breeding of the fighting-cock," like several
of his angling predecessors, he would likely have
crossed on till he had produced midden fowls to
have beaked it with eagles; but luckily he had
not the cock-fighting propensity. And what,
after all, was fishing in the *Dove* and *Stowr*, with
paddock baits, for geds and gudgeons, to the run of a
salmon in the silver Tweed ?   I wonder how he would
have looked if he had been brought here by rail, and
set down below our *Hare Crag* with a twenty feet
rod in hand, and seen and felt a twenty pound salmon
snap down his fly to the bottom, and there hold it
as firmly as if it had been fixed to the rock in
the deep, with only a little tremulous indication of
life at both ends : and then, again, when the sudden
bolt up the strong current took place, with the dash out

at the top, showing the broad, silvery, and glancing side to the light of day! To imagine the odds between old Isaac and Dr Johnson, brought perforce into that particular position is ludicrous enough, and can only be exceeded by the next supposed image of seeing both snug at supper in their Inn, with the same salmon presented in his next glorious altitude, well-dressed, and set round with sprigs of parsley and piggins of sauce. Who of the two would have said the grace? I think that duty would have devolved on old Isaac of necessity, as the doctor's mouth-watering would have prevented articulation. The doctor, on returning thanks, would assuredly have acknowledged the blessing as sent by God's merciful providence to his maw, by whatever method of stick and string it had been captured.

*   *   *   *   *   *

Since publishing the first edition of this dissertation on River Angling in 1840, I have written out some recent observations and corrections, which will be found under their proper headings in the present edition; as this will likely be the last opportunity I can have of doing so, or of noting further experience. My remarks will be found truly practical—a description of my own successful practice and personal observation, regardless of other eyes and au-

thors.   Indeed, I hardly quote another author,
as the late ones possess nothing new to me, and
the old are hardly at all applicable to our Scotch
rivers.

I conceive it better to make particular mention
only of the best standard flies, with the manner of
dressing and using them, than to give a detailed
description of infinite and inferior varieties.   I will,
therefore, give only useful directions, divested of all
the unnecessary discussions and superfluity of frivolous anecdotes, which have hitherto tended to
swell the bulk of treatises on this subject.   Thus
will also be avoided all insignificant and endless
enumeration and invention of names to flies, which
rather tend to bewilder the reader's imagination
than prove instructive to the individual desirous of
practical information.

Should the style of language be considered not
sufficiently perspicuous, the reader will be lenient
when assured that he has got the very best style the
writer can possibly afford from thirty shillings' worth
of scholastic education.

SALMON FLIES.

Salmon will occasionally take any fly of a hundred shades of variety; and often, in the most promising hour of weather and water, will, without any understood cause, disregard all kinds whatever. They are therefore accounted more capricious creatures than we might consider them, were we better acquainted with their appetites and habits, their incitements, and likely other sensibilities dependent upon certain unknown combinations of atmospheric influence, by which we ourselves feel often affected, yet cannot, with all our boasted philosophy, define how or why.

No one can say that he has ever seen any insect or fly frequenting the surface of our waters which in any respect nearly resembles those with which we angle most successfully for salmon.* Therefore, an

---

* One insect that occasionally frequents river margins occurs to us as resembling some salmon flies—the dragonfly; only it does not appear till about mid-summer, a season when almost no salmon are in the fly-casts. Dragonflies show all the colours of the rainbow, and the largest are as long as a medium sized salmon hook. We do not mean to say, however, that salmon ever take the artificial fly thinking it the dragonfly; but the insect decidedly resembles some of the lighter dressed salmon hooks.—[EDR.]

imitation of nature is not in this, as in general cases, the ground on which the salmon-fly angler can possibly proceed; since, in this pursuit, he is left in a great measure to his own fancy; until from long experience he has discovered the combinations of fur and feather with which he finds himself, or perceives others, most generally successful.

From experience in dressing flies for other people, and frequent angling for my own recreation, I have long ago decided on the flies which the salmon seems generally to prefer. These I have reduced into six distinct kinds; and on investigating why these should generally be more successful, they will be found to embrace all the clearly marked distinctions of the leading character of the flies in common use. For instance, suppose you were to collect all the flies generally used on the Tweed, they would, at first sight, present the appearance of an endless confusion of variety; yet I am convinced you could not classify them into above six, or at most seven distinct kinds, in which the decided principle of all the vague variety of colour in fur, wool, and feather, would be found to concentrate,   Consequently, the best known materials, wrought into the best practical combinations for proper effect, will be found to constitute the half dozen flies I shall here endeavour to describe ; and this upon the same principle as the infinite variety of lines diffused throughout the floral creation may be referable into the pristine colours of the rainbow.

FIRST FLY.

FIRST FLY.—A black body of fine soft cow-hair, or other fur (in consistence like that from the flank of a cow or kyloe), with a tuft of yellow floss, silk, or fine worsted wool, for tail, and a little red, green, or deep orange twisted close round the root of the tail-tuft. Then roll gold twist thread round the body, about an eighth part of an inch distance between the folds, and prick the hair out with a pin, and shade it as equally over the gold thread as possible, giving it a fine soft hackle appearance; and give a turn or two of dark orange, or rather red, round the shoulder, close below the root of the wings. A grey or bright mottled turkey feather use for wings, either from the tail or from behind the quill feathers in the wing of the fowl, according to size and circumstance, and have the mottle or speckle equally bright on both sides of the feather.

If a smaller sized hook :—where the pile of the feather is sufficiently long to extend the length of the fly's body, take one of four feathers from each side of the back of the drake immediately above the wing.

Some prefer the mallard, insisting that its feathers are softer. I prefer the tame drake, as its feathers are soft enough, far more distinctly mottled, and more varied in light and dark shades of colour, to be used according to the state of water and other circumstances. The grey feather of the argus, or that of the silver pheasant, with its fine white bars across, is perhaps as good as either turkey or drake. A small feather lies below the wing of the snipe, about an inch and a half long, of a beautiful light grey, very well adapted for a large-sized fly, by tying the two corresponding feathers on entire for the pair of wings, adjusting the length by the body of the fly. The wings should never be so long as to project over the tail-tuft, and they may be put on unbroken, with the upper sides of the feather kept outermost, and lying along not too widely expanded from the body of the fly. Slight variations may occasionally be used with effect. As, for instance, dark blue wool for body, or water-rat fur, over which roll a cock hackle, preferring the kind which are black half way along from the root and red towards the top, the colour as bright on both sides as can possibly be got. In low water and bright weather, the light grey wings should be supplanted by others of a bright brown hackle, even as deep as the colour of the woodcock-wing. The bittern's is an excellent wing of this kind, and large enough for any size of summer fly.

The second fly has in all respects the very same body as the first, the only variation being in the wings, which have what we technically term *a white-top*. This is a black or dark brown feather, with a little white on the top, from the tail of the turkey for the largest size of fly, or from the rump above the tail for the smaller sizes ; the feathers being smaller every row as they ascend upwards from the tail to the back of the fowl. Of this last rump feather, which is alike in length of pile on both sides of the stem, you have the advantage of forming the pair of wings with the greatest facility, by cutting with the point of a pen-knife the stem of the feather at the exact breadth of the wings intended for your fly, which are thus more easily tied on unbroken, as most wings had best be. Those white-topped feathers, the lower part of which are of a glossy black, are preferable; and the white top had best not exceed three eighths of an inch, and even three sixteenths make a fine fly of a small size ; and if the hook is a large size, I would not disapprove of three colours in the wing—say a dun white below (as they often are found), black in the middle, and the white-top nodding over above.

THIRD FLY.

The third fly has the same body and tail as the former, with white wings; but prefer those of a pale or French white, that is of a light buff or yellowish tinge. This feather is got also from the white or cream coloured turkey's tail or rump. But the wings of such a fly should by no means be broad or full, only a few piles of feather in each wing being requisite.

This fly is preferable in cold spring fishing, particularly in heavy water. It is likely that this wing catches the salmon's eye more readily in deep or sullied water, as he will come up to it boldly when he will rise to no other. If the wings of this fly are too broad and flashy, you may readily raise a fish; but on a closer sight he will reject it and pass it untouched. Therefore give only as much wing as will render the fly perceptible to the fish from the bottom of the deep water; anything more will give it an unnatural appearance to him on a nearer inspection.

FOURTH FLY.

The fourth fly, in many cases the best, is altogether of a dun colour, body and wings. Although fox and other furs and mohairs, may be used for the body of this fly, with a hackle rolled over it, still I prefer fine woolly cow hair from the flank of a dun-coloured cow or outfield kyloe. This, with a little gold twist rolled round the body, to give it an insect appearance, and the hair picked out to fall softly in a half shading over it, is, when well done, on all colours of fly, better than cock hackles. The proper dun colour is not easily described. It seems to partake of brown and white, a shade of red and yellow, with the slightest tinge of silvery grey, and a yellow tail tufted up with a speck of red. The wings are best when of the same colour, or at least as nearly so as possible, but prefer such as have a tendency to whiteness on the top. These may best be had from the tail or rump of a dun turkey, a fowl precious to a Tweed salmon fisher.

FIFTH FLY.

The body of the fifth fly is made of the dark grey fur of the hare's lug, mixed with the least quantity of bright red or deep orange mohair, or rather fine pig's wool (if fine pig's wool can be got with a tuft of yellow), over which, at the insertion of such tail or tuft, give a turn or two round of red worsted, mohair, or pig's wool. No hook requires the dresser to be more painstaking in dubbing the body. The

4

fur used is the fine dark grey on the front of the
hare's lug, where the fur is below a quarter of an
inch long. This fur requires to be pirled* with the
thumb and fore finger, along with the waxed thread.
This gives it a sort of felting-on with the thread
when you are rolling it round the shank of the hook.
Still continue the motion of twisting while rolling
it round. As you cannot come over the hook again
with a second coat, it requires the necessary thickness to be done up at once over, and afterwards
adjusted with pickings and trimmings, which can be
better done with a small awl, having a handle, than
a pin. If the hook is of a large size, I approve of a
fine gold twist rolled around it, and a short bristled
hackle laid in the lee of the tinsel. But as this is
a fly more adapted to summer waters, and therefore
seldom requires to be dressed on the largest size of
hook, a hackle may be dispensed with. I have had
best success without a hackle, when the short fur was
neatly picked up to shade a little over the tinsel, the
tinsel only a one-third ply of the gold twist. For
the largest size of this fly, the ears of the roe-deer
are, by my friend elsewhere alluded to, preferred to
the hare's lug, as being a beautiful grey, and making
a lovely body, either with or without a hackle. Of

* *Anglice* Twisted.

course these furs, like all others, ought to be gathered while the animal has its winter coat on.

The long tuft feathers on the head of the lapwing make a first-rate hackle for this, or for any low-water fly, as the feather is long enough to lap often round, and very fine and short in the bristle. A wing from the bright mottled feathers of the drake is the best adapted for this body, taking those of the lighter shade for the heavier water, and darker struck ones as the water falls into clearness, until on the smallest summer fly you may prefer a clear brown woodcock wing, which, from an old bird, is decidedly preferable to that from a younger one. But, as the woodcock wing will answer only a very small salmon fly, apply to the bittern, or to a beautiful, dark, drake back-feather for wing.

I recommend here nothing but what I have personally proven to my full satisfaction.

SIXTH FLY, OR THE MAULE FLY.

My sixth fly I will distinguish by calling it the *Maule* fly, which, though not much different from my first fly, yet is in some points peculiar ; and principally in this, that Mr Maule hardly ever used any but this one kind, only varying the size of it from the largest size of hook (generally used on heavy water) down to the very smallest, little above the size of a large trout fly, say No. 9 or 10 of Adlington's. From the least to the largest size this fly was made up of a medium colour of sky-blue fine wool, with small pallid tinsel, or no tinsel, and a very peculiar cock hackle : to wit, black from the root up along the middle stem to fully half the length, then running into red out to the top—and a yellow or light orange tuft for tail—the wings of a soft mottled turkey tail feather, dark grey. A wing feather, however favourably mottled, he considered too stiff and unpliable. Mr Maule in dressing this fly differed from my mode of dressing. Instead of cutting off the pair of wings from the feather, and putting them on unbroken in the web, he tore them from the stem, then equalising their points, pirled them between his thumb and finger till well mixed; then tied them on with their tops laid back, adjusting the roots with knife or scissors. He then folded them forward and divided them equally; and next, by several crossings of the fine thread, tied them solidly in position, and trimmed off the fly. This fly he sunk by means of a blue silk casting line, which he had pointed off with five or six lengths of gut. In throwing this line he beat everybody ; and from his art in sinking it, he brought it to near the fish on his lair at the bottom; and by these means he was more successful generally than any other fisher. I had long heard of Mr Maule and his success, and always with the warmest admiration, as a first-rate fisher, and a first-rate man; but I never met him till some years after my publication on angling had appeared—then I found him the man in every true sense of the name, and the gentleman in its every legitimate sense.

We have lost him now, several years since. Why should the true lovers of angling and worth not have him monumented at Boldside Boathouse, where he often lodged with the fisherman? I dare say the laird of Gala would not refuse the stance, were the idea respectfully represented. Were the rocks yonder mine, I would invite the monument; because we have had no fisher since the time of old Walton and Cotton characteristically comparable to the late Mr Maule.

MISCELLANEOUS OBSERVATIONS
ON SALMON FLIES.

For occasional variation of the three first flies, the body may be made of peacock's herl, using as many piles rolled round together as will produce the proper thickness of body. In this case a fine dark hackle is necessary to give it the proper appearance. Such hackle laid round close in behind the gold twist, produces a neat effect, besides being thus saved by the gold thread from the teeth of the fish, which are apt to cut the hackle unless so protected. I prefer all hackles rather short in the bristle than long. Those fine half-black, half-red hackles, so common with us forty years ago, seem now to be out of fashion among our barn-door fowls; few of the present colours are bright throughout; the inside is generally of a dirty pale yellow. Also, the real black are now changed to white near the root; still, with some trouble proper ones may be here and there found. Cocks of the game breed produce the best hackles for fly dressing, generally being longer in the feather,

and shorter in the bristle, than those of the common
fowl.

I am not fond of broad shining tinsel in any
case, except occasionally in deep, dark, cold, winter
water, and then I prefer gold to silver twist, as it is
not so showy ; and, except on a large hook in dark
water, a silk thread, or a piece of gut rolled round
the body, to give the fly a maggot appearance, is
perhaps preferable to any twist or tinsel. In very
clear water, and fine weather, I consider all sorts of
tinsel unnecessary.

Pig's wool when it can be got well dyed and of
various colours is preferable for tails and tufts to
mohair and worsted, being of a brighter dye and
more determined colour in the water.

Much has been said of late of Irish flies, made
(like butterflies) of parrot, golden-pheasant, and other
bright fancy feathers; and even broad clear tinsel,
with rough, red, blue, and white hackles, has been
occasionally used on the Tweed with success. Hence,
inexperienced fishers are very unwilling to believe in
the general propriety of sober coloured flies. Yet,
if the matter be observed and considered, it will be
found resolvable into the principle of *light colours
for deep dark waters.* Partial success in high or
agitated waters is an exception to the general rule,

and does not constitute a gaudy fly a standard one for ordinary pool and stream fishing. Besides, people often decide hastily in approbation of those flies with which they raise salmon, whether the fish touch their hook or not, thinking he has missed his bite. I think very differently in such a case. The fish lies quite at ease in the water, even in the gully-rush of a cauld dyke-slap, and on a glance of a fly moving over him, will sweep up in soft easy motion, and follow it round the curve it describes with a discerning eye; and on resolving to seize it, he will not miss his bite once in twenty cases; but when not pleased with the fly, he will shy off, at which instant you may often perceive a back-fin, or half the web of his tail flap above the surface, or he will throw himself indignantly out of the water, and sinking back with easy motion, return again to his old lair, his chosen spot on the rock at the bottom of the river. By overlooking an angler from an eminence, we may see many fish rise coolly and examine his fly, of which he himself has no perception, not being in a position to perceive any that do not touch his fly or come up above the surface.

In regard to flies generally, either for salmon or trout, I have in practice found it beneficial to attend principally to a natural proportion of parts, which it

is not easy to give or to receive a very proper idea
of by mere description, and of which an individual
can only acquire a correct notion from personal experience and attention to those in general practice.
For instance, instead of a full dress, starched-looking
fly, give it rather upon the whole as much of a
modest, maggot appearance as possible. The wings
should lie at seeming ease, less than half extended
from the sides of its body, which body is the better
of looking somewhat caterpillar-like.

I do not allege that the materials of fur and feather
here specified, are the very best of any to be found
in the range of nature for the effects I intend to be
produced : they are only the best I have found convenient, being our own local product. What I
advise relates more properly to the general combinations of the colours, shape, and size of the fly, as
suitable to the high or low state of the water, than
to the particular materials by which such a com-
bination may be best effected. For instance, several
foreign birds and fowls—such as the Bengal and
other kinds of bustard, the pencilled and silver
pheasants—produce beautiful feathers, particularly
of the black-and-white, barred, and mottled kinds.
There are many English fowls, the plumage of some
hundreds of which I have seen (preserved by a gentle-

man in Warwickshire), and several of which I noted as being of a superior kind for wings to my favourite flies. The drake of the *pocheral*, or great red-headed *widgeon*, I would prefer as wings for my first fly. The *gadwall* or *greywill*—the saddle feathers of his back, and those over his groin, are also excellent for the same purpose.

The web or sheet part of the wing of the great grey gull, as well as his tail, is splendid for the wings of very light salmon flies, grey in place of pure white —this for my third fly. The *greater gull* and common *sea-maw* have beautiful feathers of an azure white still rather superior for the same fly. Then the *cock shoveller* has feathers on the saddle and over his loins charming for a fine dun fly, and his tail is valuable for beautiful light speckled wings. The buzzard and kite are alike excellent for light dun wings for a large fly; and for a duller shade there is a speckled feather in the spread of the pea-fowl's wing finely adapted for a hook of large or middle size, and easily tied on without separating the pile; but with a little trouble in the selection, the turkey produces nearly all the varieties of mixture and shades really necessary.

In collecting and preserving feathers, I would recommend to select merely the feather, or that part of it that is of positive use, stripping off the refuse which tends to foster moths, by which three fourths of all the best collected feathers are generally soon destroyed. In a box two inches deep, and eighteen long, by twelve broad, I can preserve all the feathers useful to dress, say ten thousand flies. To preserve them clean and right, tumble them all out frequently, say every three months, on a newspaper, brush out the box, and then lift every feather singly, clean it by stripping it between your thumb and finger, and replace it in the box. This will prevent moth-bites, and keep all tight and clean.

I consider it unnecessary to vary these flies in hope of success; only, be particular in adapting the size of the hook to the state of the water, as from the time the water has fallen in from a flooded state to a fishing size, and thence down to the lowest size of pure summer clearness, it requires not the *colours* or the *form* of the flies to be varied, so much as the *size*, which gradually diminish from the largest salmon hook down to the smallest, even to the size of a trout bait-hook, No. 10 of Adlington's; and, when trouting in low clear water, a salmon will often take your large trout fly, such as a March brown—after all forms of salmon flies have floated over him in vain. With my spring trout fly, No. 7 of

Adlington's, I have killed a fish fifteen pounds
weight. They feed in the low water exactly as the
trout does, and with caution and patience these flies
often yield amazing sport.

But the point most essentially necessary to be
clearly understood in angling, and which, however simple, seems generally to be overlooked even by writers
on the subject, although the most easily perceived in
the practice, as well as on the slightest glance at the
philosophy of the case, is this :—The salmon lies the
whole day stationary on his chosen spot on the rock, at
the bottom of the water, four, six, or eight feet deep,
from which situation he must perceive the fly on
the surface before he ascends to seize it ; therefore,
it must be of size and colour to catch his eye through
that medium of water less or more agitated, as well
as discoloured by earthy particles.   Hence the main
difficulty of ascertaining the exact size of fly, wing
and body, first to catch his observation, and excite
him to rise, and yet not to exceed the appearance of
nature on his nearer approach.   I have often known
a fish in deep water rise three times successively at
a fly of a very full white wing without effect, and
when I diminished the breadth of each wing by half,
he seized it greedily on the fourth rise.   On this
principle is grounded the main reason why every

fisher succeeds better on his own water than a stranger, from his local knowledge of the depth and eddy, rock and gravel, of every *cast*, pool and stream. He knows from daily experience the size and colour of the fly requisite for each, according to the state of water, whether or not he is at all able to explain the matter.

Deep water, either in pool or rapid, generally requires a fly of a larger size than more shallow pools and streams, even on the same day ; and that without change of sky, wind, weather, or water. In heavy water, or in fishing over a deep *cast*, I prefer going over it first with the largest or brightest fly I suppose at all likely, say a large size of my third fly ; this may catch his eye and engage his attention. Should this not raise him, or should he rise and pass the fly, then try him with one a size or two smaller, or a little more sober in colour, which he will likely then take. On the contrary, in low pure water, when beginning to go over a *cast*, use your smallest or sober coloured fly first, and if he do not rise to it, then go over the cast again with one a size larger, or a shade brighter.

An experienced, good fisher, even on a strange river, may conceive pretty nearly the spot where a fish will lie, according to circumstances—the state of the water, or the curve of the surface, in pool, rapid, or eddy ; but no description is of avail in giving an idea of this, as the skill can only be acquired by experience.

Since Irish flies were first tried in the Tweed, that is within thirty years back,* they have been, if not gaining in favour, at least keeping a distinguished place on " the face of the waters," and have got a standing amongst the fly fashions of the age. This certainly shows that they are somehow cognate to our old legitimate Tweed flies. Yet that the success has been greater with them upon the whole, than in a corresponding length of time previously with the old flies alone, may be disputed. That more fish were caught in the thirty years before they were introduced is no argument against them, all other casualties duly considered. We are, therefore, obliged to hesitate in a decision for or against preference of either. On a broad view, my own conception of the matter is this, that Irish flies may be found preferable in muddy, dark waters, being constructed of bright colours—golden pheasant, yellows, oranges, &c.—and that newly come fish see them more quickly, while the water is yet a little discoloured from the soil in a flooded river, and from this cause take them

Now fifty years.—[EDR.]

more briskly than flies of darker hues. New run grilse certainly prefer them, as I have found those always fonder of a bright fly (with glittering tinsel and showy colours, even white hackles) than heavy old-run salmon are. Heavy fish keep more in the deep water, and never take the fly well till the river has fallen low and clear, and then sober coloured flies please them best, as likely agreeing better with the low clear state of the water. Clear or coloured water will account for one half of the whole phenomena. In discoloured water bright feathers appear as dim as sober colours appear in the clear.

It is long since we were satisfied that the living type of what we call our salmon flies is not found in fresh waters or produced there, either on the land or in the river. For what, then, the salmon take our flies has been the continued unanswered question.

From a late brown study on this subject (perhaps the fiftieth I have caught myself in in as many years), I have been pleasurably aroused by the present of a valuable book, from a kind gentleman, entitled "The Earn, its Legends and Fly Fishing," by the Rev. Henry Newland, rector and vicar of Westbourn. In this book, among a variety of pleasing observations and well told anecdotes, the author, supposes the *shrimp* to be the natural prototype to which our artificial salmon flies form an accidental resemblance, in the structure as well as in their jerking motions, caused by their attachment to the line in the current of water.

Having never then seen a shrimp, dead or alive, I could not blame myself in not having detected it as decidedly the true prototype which I had so long been in imaginary search of, being always convinced that it must be a marine production, and very common on feeding shoals in the sea Had I ever seen a shrimp, I think I might have caught up the idea at once; and now what a variety of proofs come in on the mind in support of the opinion, which is no longer an *opinion* with me but a decided fact, as all past observation, from experience and analogy, rushes in, confirmatory of the truth of the parson's observation. One point which goes far in proof of this opinion, is this, that every good fisher must have observed that his fish bites surest at the fly when well sunk in the water, say to mid-depth or so; and it is also a sure sign of a fisher knowing his business from experience when we see him endeavouring to sink his fly well, in place of making a novice-like effort to keep it on the surface. In fact, I think I may be correct in advising to even add a little weight occasionally in a deep and strong current, say a grain or two of shot, a gut

length or so from the fly, the same as is used in minnow and worm fishing.*   This is one of those con-
ceptions of which we feel certain without having put
it to clear proof.   Whoever will try it I am convinced will succeed.   Large old salmon do not readily
take the fly in heavy or soiled water; the main reason is likely this, that they keep low in the water,
resting frequently, like other heavy old creatures.
This rest they take on the bottom rock or gravel,
and do not prowl in mid-depth as the grilse, being
young, sportively do.   Hence, the grilse meeting
with your bright fly, see and seize it, while it is not
seen by the salmon below.   By the time the water
has again fallen in to the low fishing size, the dull
flies, what we call the legitimate Tweed flies, are
again found bright enough, and mainly in request.
I have only twice in fifty-seven years seen something

* We may mention a case favouring Younger's idea on this point.
Some years ago in the Tweed, a few miles from Kelso, an old and experienced salmon angler found in the early spring that the fish would
not rise, though he tried them with all sorts and sizes of flies; and
it occurred to him that perhaps the salmon in dull and rough waters
might not be able to see his flies, or that they would not move or rise
from the coldness of the atmosphere. He therefore got the fisherman
to dress him a large fly, on the shank of which he had strapped small
beads, with hackles between.   The weight of beads made the hook
sink deeply in the water, and the result was that the gentleman for
a week or so had first-rate sport, although anglers on other neigh-
bouring waters were doing almost nothing.   In summer waters,
however, this gentleman, like other anglers, sinks his fly by its own
weight and the manner in which he works his rod.—[EDR.]

5

apparently the reverse of this, which might at first sight have posed a fishing philosopher to account for. In a heavy late autumn flood, in the second week of October, a run of large *grey schule* fish came up, literally stocking the river, while yet running black and full. For three or four days they seemed all keeping near to the surface, tumbling up everywhere incessantly, to near the very bordering grass, and seizing at sight any large fly you might throw in ; but yet [being] on the run upward, they would not settle till the water should fall low. This does not fully account for the whole phenomenon, as more were still moving on from the sea, till in a few days they became sobered down and would not rise to a fly ; but when the water had fallen to a mean fishing size, they fell to be fished for in the ordinary way. We may observe that if our parson's bright yellow fly—which he names from his own profession, *The Parson*—is his studied imitation of a shrimp, copied from the type (and we say the salmon take it for a shrimp), then what do the salmon take other flies for ? certainly, as well all for shrimps—black, blue, brown, and dun as well as yellow. This holds at all points to our purpose, in proof that it is the shrimp that salmon flies of all colours are taken for. The bright golden flies of the *Earn*, and the darker flies of the *Tweed*, must all be imitations of *shrimps*, though unwittingly so designed.

The living parson has copied a fly from one bright yellow shrimp, found it a killer, and named it after himself; but from a handful or two of shrimps I shall pick out a dozen, in which his six pictured favourite Earn flies and my half-dozen of Tweed ones, will be found a resemblance as near as if imitated intentionally; and these may be even more like when moving in the water. And shrimps are as varied in their colours as are a flock of fancy pigeons,* and of all sizes too, the same as we make salmon flies.

It would appear then, that all along in making up our salmon flies, we have, by a repetition of experimental trials, been arriving at effect, without adverting to the proper type as the cause. Who of those who in primitive ages " cast angle in the brooks" would first conceive the notion of what we call the salmon fly (like no living fly that has been seen), or what might suggest such idea to their imagination, must remain, as it has hitherto been, undeclared, and unremarked, even in tradition. It would be a curi-

---

* We doubt if John is entirely correct as to the colour of shrimps. We have many a time caught them, both on dull and sunny days, and their colour always seemed the same or nearly so. When the sun shone we occasionally noticed a light or faint shade of steel blue upon some of them, but so faint that the natural colour was still the predominating one, namely, that of sea sand.—[EDR.]

ous experiment for some one—how amused he would feel at his first success. Whether an ancient philosopher, or a neat herd boy, is of little consequence. And now when we do believe the shrimp is the small marine creature to be imitated (instead of some unknown fly of the air), and in consequence, in making up our deceptions, strive to copy that little fish more closely, yet in this we may not succeed better than by holding to our old experience.

From examination of the shrimp dry in our hand, along with the best imitation we may be able to make of it, we might be misled in our judgment on the matter, from the want of being able to examine it with the eye of a salmon through a salt water medium, where the effect of colour, shape, and motion, may give a very different appearance; and hence, after having acknowledged our conviction of the exactitude of our similitude, may yet be led to prefer our old fashion from the mere accidence of eventual success. This is to say that our chance imitation, formed upon the principle of success in repeated trials, may be as true a resemblance as a more closely designed imitation might ensure. Yet still it is a curious consideration that, in this case, so much imagination has been let loose in conjecturing what living type these flies might be the imitation of, and no one till now should have stumbled upon this salt sea shrimp. We are now making as renowned a fish of him as if he were actually the great " salt-sea shark." He is a most active little fellow, with his score of limbs, arms, oars, feelers, and feathered tail, all spread in action. On minute observation our salmon flies resemble this shrimp more than any other creature we wot of, either on land or in water : their various size, indicating youth or age, the form of body with its appendages, and the different colours they assume, agreeably to the reflection in light or shade, like the pheasant's or pigeon's neck. Then, observe this creature in its own element moving through the variety of its exercitations, its limbs thrown abroad like a bird's wings in air, and feet moving as swimming in mid-depth of water, its contractions and expansions, as it draws in the hinder part of its body, and strikes back with its horizontally spread tail in acceleration of progression. Then see the salmon at ease below, his ever-awake eye alert on the watch for prey, as well as against surprise. Now he shoots forward like a feathered dart, or, nosing out on the prowl, snaps up the shrimp as the swallow takes flies in the upper element.

What a picture does nature everywhere present,

if we had eyes calculated to see through her grand *media* and take in the minutiæ as well as the expanse of her canvas.

These shrimps are everywhere acknowledged a very nutritious, as well as a savoury dish at table. No wonder then, that the salmon which leave our rivers in the spring in a poor meagré state should so soon again get into grand condition ; and that the slabby white muscle of his body grows red, rich, and incomparable, as the digested substance of five hundred shrimps a day may make it in a month.

Be this as it may, we are certain that salmon take our fly for something that must nearly imitate what they know to be their food. Or suppose them to have been confined to a situation where they have never seen such species, they would yet seize our fly on sight, as a cat would a mouse, from an intuitive impression that it is their natural prey. We may rest assured, however, that it is not a fly of the air, nor a fresh water production that the salmon take it for, as such have never been observed by the fishers of late generations, nor recorded by any of the former ; yet, we may not even now alter its name, but call it still the salmon fly.

TROUT FLIES,

NATURAL AND ARTIFICIAL.

Before proceeding to give my selection of trout flies, I would wish to observe how these flies are bred, and the successive appearances they present in their change from one state to another, which will assist you to account upon philosophical principles for various phenomena occurrent in angling, which tend to confuse the ideas of superficial observers.

If in the middle of winter you lift a stone from the bottom of the river, you may perceive on the under side of it numbers of small cases, formed of mud-particles, cemented by a glutinous substance into a consistency like brown paper; by pressing this case you will see that it contains a dark green maggot, or chrysalis of the future water-fly.* These are

* We have lifted hundreds of stones both in winter and early spring for the purpose of examining the water flies in their maggot state, and even to very small pebbles they are often sticking numerously. The family is greatly varied, both in size and shape, and each kind has its own peculiar covering or outer skin. One or two of the kinds have a somewhat uncanny look, and few but Waltonians would care about handling them.—[EDR.]

in myriads, and constitute a portion of the food of trouts throughout the winter, as they do in their more fully developed state when winged in the summer. On 23d November, 1837, from the stomach of a trout about half-a-pound weight, I counted out three hundred of these maggots all in the skins, many of them still retaining the appearance of life.

The genial fine weather in early spring brings forth a portion of these maggots every fresh sunny hour, just as they come into a state of forwardness toward the maturity of their existence. Having left their habitation on the stone, they float for some time enclosed in a second tough film, within which their wings lie in one single fold, and from which they creep out by degrees, leaving this last vestment a floating wreck. So soon as extricated, their wings spring erect, shewing them off the finished, lovely, gentle denizens of air.*

Not a more delectable half-hour's amusement have

* A friend who has been a keen angler for fifty years, gave us the following information :—An old man of his acquaintance (but not an angler) came to him one day and said he had something to tell him that he thought very curious. He had been sitting in the sunshine close by the river, when he saw what he thought a small bit of brown moss rise from the bottom of the water to the surface. He kept looking at it for a few seconds, when he thought it began to move. Presently a small fly stood erect upon it, then spread out its wings and flew off ; and one fly after another continued to do the same until the brown speck disappeared, it having been a cluster of water-flies.—[EDR.]

I ever had in my life long (except in sweethearting when young), than in lifting one of those aurelia from the stream, and sitting down with it on the palm of my hand in the sun, till it put out its feelers, and drew itself by degrees from its envelopment. Then its wings sprang erect, shewing it off as tenderly-pure as a vision of thought; and when dried, it mounted in its new element, to delight its hour or its day in the pleasures of a new state of joyous existence.

Though some species of the water fly have been considered ephemeral, I do not think any of them are exactly so; as they continue to flutter about the bushes, where you may beat them out in thousands in a cold morning, and when brought home to the windows they will live for several days. After they have risen from their maggot state at the bottom of the water, to the most perfect winged portion of their existence, they swim and flutter on the surface till they have gone through all the operations necessary to the continuance of their species, dropping their eggs on the surface, which, being of more specific gravity than water, sink gradually: and wherever the current of water may leave them at the bottom, which is most generally on a ford, they settle and adhere by an emitted gluey substance to the under edges of the stones, where they are carried in by the current; and where, from the sediment of the river, they attach the material particles proper to form the case in which we find them there contained, and which, by some operation of the insect, is formed into a proper fitting sheath for its body. Here it lies snug, with its black head and fore feet, or feelers, peeping out on the sweet light of life,* dining like a young emperor on the rich, delicate, minute animalculæ of which the water is pregnant.

Trout angling is very different from salmon angling; because, the trout when feeding on flies swims about in middle-water, or rather nearer to the surface, picking and choosing the fly most agreeable to his taste. For instance, in a summer flood, when the river begins to subside, you may perceive on the yet brown muddy water a variety of flies, of many kinds and colours, floating down the current, and the trout rejecting all the gay profusion as they pass, and selecting one kind (probably a dark coloured midge fly), no doubt just as carefully as he does in the clearest water—when circling round his pool with an easy motion, you may observe him darting forward to scan the coming fly, which he

---

* The cradle-skin of a large number of these maggots is quite close, and these can, of course, neither put out head nor feet.—[EDR.]

likely may reject, springing aside to seize another of a kind which he approves.

As the trout are feeding on these insects in all states, both at the bottom and as they ascend to the surface, no wonder that people sometimes catch a few trouts with very ill-formed flies, even without wings altogether. Yet this is not a sufficient reason why you should not have a fly formed to give as much as possible the shape, colour, and appearance of the natural fly in its state of fullest perfection; and, for this purpose, I will here briefly give you my selection of trout flies, imitated so as best to promote general success throughout the season. I shall reduce them to only a few in my description, as I have found only a very few really necessary in my general practice.

But first allow me to observe, that if you go out a-trouting about nine or ten o'clock on a mild March or April day, you may thrash away perhaps an hour or two without seeing a natural fly, or a trout rise. At last, unexpectedly, you will hook a trout with your flies carelessly half-sunk in the water; and before you have landed it, you will perceive the trouts all in a plunge—nothing but heads and tails flapping amidst myriads of pretty large flies, which, according as the light strikes them, may cause the surface of the middle current to assume a reddish-brown appearance when seen in the distance. On a nearer inspection, you may conceive that they might be best imitated by the dark grey of a hare's lug for body, and brown speckled woodcock wings—which most fishers positively decide on using in preference to other material, never considering that hare's-ear fur is darker coloured when wet; and of which, therefore, from experience, I disapprove, preferring the body rather of the shortest, or belly part, of water-mouse fur, teased up together with an equal proportion of yellow fine wool or mohair. This mixture shows of a tarnished green colour, and when in your hand looks too light for the body of the natural fly, but when wet, must to the trout have the nearest resemblance, as with it you will have most success throughout the spring months.

First take of Adlington's hooks (round bend), No. 7, to form your pair of flies (or whatever maker's hooks you may approve, but let them be of that size); make the wings of the one fly of the lighter coloured part of the woodcock wing feather, or rather prefer the softer and lighter coloured feathers from the middle of the web of the partridge wing. Make the other fly, the blae one of your pair, with either a starling wing, a bunting, or mistletoe thrush. I cannot decide as to which of all these is the best. Let the body of both flies be made of the shortest of the water-rat fur, that which grows nearest the belly, and has a yellowish grey lustre on the surface; this mix up with an equal proportion of yellow worsted wool or mohair (dyed pig's wool is preferable, when it can be got fine enough) well teased together. With this make your fly, body and wings, fully as large, upon the whole, as the fly you imitate (in earliest spring I sometimes use No. 8), and fish on with this pair, using no variation whatever, from early spring down to the setting in of fine weather, about the end of April. Then the fly of which this is the imitation is succeeded by one of a size smaller, or rather more slender, and the least shade lighter in colour of body and transparency of wing. In England the first of these flies is called the *March Brown*, the second the *Pale Yellow Dun.*

In ordinary seasons, this last fly comes up about the end of April, or beginning of May, and continues for a month or more in main request, making still a secondary fly all down the summer; and when it comes first on it is the chief object of trout, in preference to the former fly, of which a few are still seen straggling on the surface. My usual imitation of this fly is with the same mixture of blue water-rat fur and pale yellow, inclining to white for body; and for wing, the most transparent feather to be got from the wing of the bunting* or the mistletoe thrush.

As these flies are tender, you may perceive them in breezy weather all dishevelled by being blown in from the ruffled surface to the sheltered eddies— their wings being dashed asunder, and spread on the water like shivered oars. In this state the trouts devour them; and from this circumstance, as well as another which I shall presently describe, a hundred vile imitations of this fly meet with partial success; while those who use such, often ignorantly aver that it is of little consequence to be nice about flies. The next best imitation of this fly (or it may be even a preferable imitation to mine, as I never used it) has the body the same as described, but small and gentle, and the wings of a small body

* Buntings are a numerous family; but from the fly he speaks of, he must mean the *yellow bunting*, the *yorlin*. To an angler with "music in his soul," the *black-headed bunting* is a river-side pest. In the early morning it follows him from bank to bank, with its whit-o, whit-o, whit-o, bringing him in mind of saw-sharpening. We once saw a brother piscator lay down his rod and commence stone-throwing with great vigour, into a bank of trees. On coming up and enquiring what he aimed at, he said he was trying to drive off a sickening bird that had "*wheetled-wheetled* there for the last half hour." This was the black-headed bunting. Strange, we have more than once seen this bird classed as a British song bird.—[EDR.]

feather from various birds (say the body feather of
the grouse, of a lightish fine freckle, stripped off the
right side), and rolled round the head, or rather neck
of your fly, in the manner of a hackle. This imi-
tates the dishevelled wings of the natural fly, and is
technically called a spider fly, and some aver that
with it they have great success, of which I have no
doubt, as I have long known it much in vogue.

I discovered my imitation of the Pale Yellow
Dun to be a killer thirty years before I really ascer-
tained its proper archetype or its name. At that
time, fishing along with a dear companion, now long
in his grave, on opposite sides of the Tweed, a little
above the *Doup Roads*, on the head of Mertoun
water, we, to prevent entanglement, took *cast about*,
our flies (though contrariwise) both alike sweeping
the same centre spot of heavy water ; and, in a circle
of within twenty yards diameter, he caught three
trouts, while, with one of the flies of my pair, I caught
fifty-four, which weighed twenty-four pounds. We
then examined that individual fly, which, in the
dressing up, I had accidentally varied from the rest
of our early spring flies, and we afterwards adopted
it as a first favourite—a successful one. It was
nearly thirty years afterwards ere I learned that this
fly (accidentally on my part) proved to be the
" Pale Yellow Dun" of English anglers.

About the middle or end of May, sooner or later, according to state of weather, a small dark blae fly appears, which may be best imitated on a small hook, No. 1 of Adlington's, or others of a similar size, the body made of the belly fur of the water-mouse— where the fur is shortest, blae-coloured, and tipped with dun—and tied with fine silk as near the same colour as possible. The wings should be made from the tip of the back feathers of the starling wing, or from any other bird's wing of a fine texture and blae colour, though I have often used those of a sparrow wing, and with success. This small fly appears on the water before the former (the second spring fly) is retired. I have preferred using one of each to form the pair, making the small blae fly the trail or end one, and the former, larger, light-coloured one, the *bob* or *dropper*, upon the consideration that the smallest fly of a pair should always be the out-end one, giving it the open chance. For days or weeks after you will take trouts alternately with each ; and observe, that though trouts may occasionally be taken at this period with flies of other descriptions than these, yet no trout that would take any other would reject these if gracefully offered. I have always hated the confusion of fishing with more than a pair of flies, and would rather nip off the dropper and fish with only one than fish with three, and be sure of more success too, as through a day or night you have no hankings or hindrance.

CURIOUS PHENOMENA.

Some curious phenomena occur in angling which may come well enough in place to relate here. In fishing either for salmon or trout, more I think depends upon the state of the atmosphere for success or non-success, than on any other single circumstance, or on all other causes taken together.

In the salmon department, we may passively observe, that often when all seems fine, and you know that salmon are in the pool or stream, and might suppose that they would just be lying ready watching for a fly; you may cast over it with all the blandishments of your art, try all known means of temptation, and even supposed new means—as well try to raise the rock he lies on ! Say that this occur twice in the day, morning and middle; yet go back about sunset, when you may likely have him up at first sight, fit to tear the rod from your hands. Now, whether he had been asleep, or had

6

not got digested his nightly or early meals, or had
merely felt lazy from some oppressive feeling, allied
to an indigestive state, such as is frequent with ourselves, is not understood ; but I rather suspect that
the real cause is from the electric state of the atmosphere, disinclining him to motion, as well as pro-
moting a dulness of appetite.

Again, in the case of the trout.   We have a fine
middle April day, we go out say at ten o'clock, the
glass at 50°, a medium state, having been pretty
steadily so for days past.   Everything looks favourable—the river just beautiful, not too much cleared-
down from the browning of a recent flood—the
atmosphere neither spiringly dry, nor drowsily heavy.
Fit up, lay on your flies, be ready for the first movement (and be alert while the movement continues),
for they cannot choose, but be all in a stir in a little.
Well, you go on, throwing out softly and dexterously,
till you have gone over a hundred, or may be three
hundred yards, up or down, of the finest water you
ever cast line on, yet not a *bell* or small circle ever
forms on the beautiful surface, except what the
soft falling of your own flies and line occasion.
You look up and see the light clouds hardly moving
on sunwards, and scarcely even whitened on the
sunny side, the least indicative sign of frost—every-

thing in perfect consonance with our notions of a good day—our own blood in free circulation to and from the heart, bearing elasticity and comfort to the nerves, and inducing even generous sympathies— the lark overhead sailing beside the light cloud, the thrush and blackbird on bush and tree, and the titmouse in the hedge below, swelling their little throats in the joy of love : why are there no flies come to the surface—they are half an hour later than I expected ? While you turn and move and stand in suspense, down floats a shower of flies literally thatching the middle current, multitudes of them whirling into creeks and eddies (say beautiful *March Browns*, bred up from the grub state on the bottom stones of the ford above the stream), and not a trout seen to flap a tail amongst them ! Why are all in motion but the fish ? No answer to this our question of thought, no solution found, the pride of our philosophy humbled. Even old father Walton and Sir Humphry Davy were aback as far as I find myself, having no reason to render for such a phenomenon. But we feel, we fret to stand inert, so keep casting on, regardless of breaking the wings of fifty living flies at every fall of our lumpish line and sham flies, on the surface, though supposed by us comparatively fine ; and having come to fish, fish we will.

I who write have gone on in this style for hours, and till nearly at the sinking in disgust of all idle earthly pursuits; and the water-carpeting of flies having imperceptibly vanished off, I could take no account of the least perceptible change of atmospheric influence, when at last a good trout would startle me with a tug at my line, half sunk from inattention. Ere I got that drawn ashore others would be plopping up here and there all around. Then I became alert and diligent, and just as I had got one carefully taken off the hook, another would have nipt down a natural fly; my flies are over the spot in a moment, up, down, or across—but a yard above his nose—and he is got fast and flouncing. No stop now takes place till my basket is full with nineteen pounds weight, just what the lid would tie down upon, and a dozen more half and whole pounders hurriedly thrown on the grass, or stuffed in my pockets with their tails flapping over. Likely then, they begin to rise more transiently when I begin to relax in persistence, getting even sick of the water side, fresh, fish smell; and, bundling up, I turn for home to see and get something of a salted taste to satisfy a well-earned appetite.

This is the description of one effect: I should like to meet with him who could give me a satisfying natural cause. In the meantime, I conceive the cause as somehow allied to electricity in some state of its negative, positive, or veering motions, but how balanced so as to produce the particular phenomenon of the flies covering the surface, and the trouts not owning them, I know no more than a philosopher.

Another morning at ten o'clock will look much the same as last in all respects, only that the first rise of flies to the surface will stir all the trout into motion; a complete flapping of heads and tails and yellow bellies tumbling up, cuffs the flies to confusion. In this case we may get a few, and only a few, for, though in feeding mood, they have such a choice before them, that our best imitations are overlooked or rejected on sight. In half an hour the hurry is over and all stilled again into a dull calm surface, till another rise of flies from the bottom, when a similar scene takes place for another half hour or so; and so on alternately down through the middle part of the day. The best thing to be recommended to an angler in such a case, is to take his place on a proper station, where he previously knows the trouts will be principally congregated; to be ready and active in picking out half a dozen or so whenever these *bestirs* are going on, and they are common on every fishing day in April, for half-hours alternately, from nine or ten till two or three afternoon.   If it continue fresh and fine, though even sunny, they will rise and take singly on till four, when you may pack up and toddle homeward, with hope of sound sleep and a still better day to-morrow.

MISCELLANEOUS OBSERVATIONS

When in bright weather and clear unruffled water you cannot succeed in throwing your flies across, or rather at a considerable angle upwards, and letting them swim down of their own accord, with no visible pull upon them, then turn your face up the water, and whether in stream or smooth pool, there throw straight up, or at such slight angle from straight up as circumstances of depth or other impediment may permit. In this way, your fly falling lightly above the feeding trout, he is apt to snap it the instant it alights ; your quick acknowledgment of feeling him being down against his mouth and body, he can hardly miss being hooked ; then lead him gently down towards you, which action alarms none above. Then proceed a step upwards, and in the next throw, breaking new water, you have a new chance.

It is easy to conceive how readily a trout is hooked in this way ; for when the fine gut is wet and pliant, the moment the fly is dropped on the surface the action of the water folds it inwards, bringing it to the trout's mouth like a natural fly afloat, and not seemingly held as hanging against the current. It is thus slack when he sucks it in, and you have only to give the slightest pull, which, being against him, gives advantage to get such a hold as settles his concern with existence. In the common way, fishing from above, the thing appears to the trout out of course, and this he perceives, from an instinct, more quickly than Sir Humphry Davy could have reasoned it from his best philosophy and knowledge of angling. Indeed, in fishing downwards in thin clear water with flies hanging against the stream, it is a wonder one should get a rise of a trout at all; and if you should, you are more likely to scart the mouths of nine, than to get hold of the tongue or lip of the tenth, which would be a chance next to a miracle. Without the method here recommended, in thin clear water, where trouts, if unalarmed, are sure to be feeding, you cannot have success—at least coming splashing down upon them in the coarse common way of proceeding in heavy water. In the fine light they fly from your line or the shadow of yourself, shy off and disown your acquaintance, and you come home like an idler, if not like an idiot, with not a trout to grace the meal for which you are hungry after such exercise.

The method above recommended of throwing aslant, or even due upwards, may to some old anglers appear sheer innovation upon old standard habits, as much so as railway trains are to their old notions of wains and carts, stage-coaches, &c. But those fishers who still adhere to the old system of fishing down or across the water, let them match themselves for a day with fishers who fish up the water, and on comparing baskets, the follower of " old saws" will gape with due wonder and dumb astonishment when he finds how much he is outstripped by the followers of " modern instances."

On the falling in of a flood the trout soon perceives, and sets out on his foray, first on the easy eddies, and sucks in the small flies in thousands, filling his stomach on dainties to repletion. Cut up a trout of a pound weight in such a time, and see in his throat and stomach ten thousand blae midge flies going into a mash amongst six or eight pars and minnows, and find that he has also been so greedy as to take your fly or minnow over all; and then don't be sorry for having *nabbed* him, and saved a million more of flies and small fish, each life as precious as his. From the stomach of a trout, of about the above weight

I have cut out six small trouts, pars, or smolts, averaging five inches long : the one first swallowed digested nearly to the bones, the last, whole and entire, still stuck in the gullet for lack of capacity in the stomach equal to the voracity of its nature. This trout took my imitation fly, over and above this gorged bellyful, by which it was caught.

The trout is not the capricious creature he has so often been represented to be; every motion and appetite of his being as exact to taste as that of any creature, bird or beast, that we wot of. There is not a mistake in the constitution of his nature and habits; all things seemingly so arise from our own misconceptions, through ignorance of his true characteristics; and be it also particularly remarked, that waterflies arise from their grub state on the bottom not at all according to months and terms, but agreeably with the state of weather. Any, and all of these kinds of flies, the spring and early summer kinds particularly, may be three weeks, or even six, later in one season than another ; and the trouts are not waiting for these flies coming to the surface, as they are always, summer and winter, helping themselves to them in the grub state, and to any particular kind of them, agreeably to their seasonable tastes, and following them to the surface as they arise, feeding upon them there also. When the flies come up thickly to the surface, as formerly described of the *March Browns*, and no trout takes them; for a trial of skill mutilate the wings of your flies by picking them off about half-middle (not cutting them); or rather by tying down the top of the wings to near the tail of the fly, which makes its appearance something like the maggot released from its first case on the bottom stone, and on its ascent to the surface. Then, as much as you can, let them sink low in the water, altogether below those flies on the surface, and you will most likely succeed in getting a few trouts, as then they take them for the grub newly come out of its case on the ground stone, and not yet quit of the silk-like film in which it is bound up—with its wings laid up in one fold, like a man with his wrists tied to his arms below his oxter, with the arm-pit joints having free motion. These pellicles, or second skins, which the flies cast off, you may see lying like chaff, covering the water edge, as drifted into coves and eddies, about the end of April and beginning of May.

When you find the trouts decidedly preferring the small fly of your pair, it being newly come on while the former is fading off, then discontinue the large *bob* one, and constitute your pair both of the small one on very fine gut.   Whatever other flies appear on the river throughout the succeeding months of July and August (nature in these months sporting her summer hues in all shapes of tinted variety, befooling our imbecile attempts at description or imitation) still continue, all along down through these months, with the same small dark flies as herein stated, with only the following occasional variation :—Let the body of one of your pair be made of a *pile* or *herl* of the peacock tail-feather, rolled round very closely to form the body in place of the blae fur, and with these you may succeed, less or more, every breezy summer day.

Although in salmon fishing we recommend a large fly for rather a heavy or dark water, that the salmon may see it from the bottom where he lies, and be tempted to rise to it, the case is completely reversed in trouting, as trout do not lie on the bottom like the salmon, but when fly-feeding, in muddy water, swim so near the surface that a quick eye may often detect their back-fins kithing above water.   This they do as much for respiration above the floating mud as for seeking food.   The smallest fly they take in its season is sought by them on the surface of the most flooded water ; and as to the fly itself, it ascends to the surface in its proper time, day and hour, whatever state the water may be in. Nature does not work in the vulgar manner of making larger flies for flooded waters, and finer and lesser ones for the low and clear.

With regard to certain states of water (dark or clear), and the colour of the fly showing more sober or bright, as the shades of light may strike and tinge it for the time being, we should not stand too stiffly upon a crotchet of opinion. We may find success though we cannot well account for it, and therefore our imitations should perhaps not be held too strictly opinionative, either in point of size or colour. We therefore may not err in sometimes holding our fly a size larger,* or a shade lighter

---

* This must, we think, have been an idea, not an experience of Younger's, otherwise he would likely have written more decidedly. He also elsewhere recommends a spring fly to be dressed larger than the fly imitated; but the summer months are not, in our opinion, favourable for angling with flies so made. The rivers are larger in March and April than in summer, and the feeding trouts also lie in deeper water, and are ever hungry and extraordinarily fond of flies in early spring; and the large fly may, from these circumstances, be more easily seen, and readily taken. But unless in early spring, or in water still very dark or muddy from a recent flood, we never knew an angler who preferred fishing with flies made larger than the natural insect. If different at all, and for clear-water fishing, most anglers like the dressed fly a trifle smaller than the living one; and we, ourselves, have many a time found a fly made up on this principle a good killer. In the streaming rippling waters, generally fished with fly in summer, the small hook cannot so readily show the cheat. The males of some of the kinds of water-flies are smaller than the females, and the difference is nowhere more noticeable than

coloured, as comparing it with the living fly when both seen together dry on our hand. In such case it may be advisable to yield to what we may find conducive to our success for the time being, rather than to stand starchly to a general principle, however supported by our ordinary philosophy.

The grand mistake of all the authors I have seen on fly fishing, is their supposition that the flies are alighting on the water from above, whereas, could they catch up the idea, or be persuaded when told, that the flies arise to the surface from the bottom where they are bred, sheets of useless speculation might be saved; such as about making your cast of flies alight softly on the surface, like living flies alighting from the air above, &c. Water flies do arise from the surface occasionally (as well as for sexual contact, like midges, bees, and birds—such as snipes and swallows,) and sometimes alight on it after. One of a thousand may do this, and on alighting be met by a ready trout; but this is rather an accidental alighting than a general case, as the trouts are really rather feeding on those arising from

in the March Browns; and from this circumstance a person dressing from a male pattern of this insect might make the artificial fly a good deal larger, and find it a killing one, but the same result, we are certain, would not follow with other flies, and in clear summer waters.—[EDR.]

the bottom upwards, while those ascending into the air are done with the water, not requiring to return.

Flies on which trout principally feed are such as are bred in water, and these having passed their ten or twelve months, in the grub state, and arisen into the full flush of their aerial term, very quickly perform the functions necessary to the continuance of their species, and leave the water as a band of newly fledged locusts leave the desert sands, flying off as may be seen, particularly in the months of April, May, and June, in myriads. I often see them on all the breezes, arise from the water and take to flight over the Tweed's banks of seventy feet high—of course unreturning. The millions of trout devour millions of flies each, still myriads are left, these flying out to the bushes and broad open downs to disport their hour, day, or term in other situations.

It must be understood that all this time, under my above receipt, you are using very fine tackle, a well balanced rod, with line to match, of a rightly calculated weight for the throw—as too light a casting line is a more grievous mistake than even too heavy—and fine gut of a water or window glass colour. The rod should be about thirteen feet—throwing out a line under easy command, say of from twenty to thirty feet, as found necessary. With

this fine light hand-piece you will nip up eight of
every ten trouts that take a *pook* at your fly thus
offered.

Touching rods we may here further observe, that
in regard to length and weight of rod and line, the
grand point is to find *balance*, by having one thing
adjusted to suit another, and all combined so as to
answer the use and habit of the individual. A
person may fish a lifetime with a short rod like a
coachman's whip, and shorter still, in such small
streams as the Ale and Kale, the Gala and Leader;
and by perseverance, and lurking about bushes and
going on his knees to hide himself and shadow, he
may be pretty successful; but still this is like shoot-
ing partridges with a pistol in place of with a fine
fowling piece.

With a rod of about fourteen feet, large enough for
having command of water, even when fishing in the
Tweed, you will also have most success in these small
streams; as with a rod well balanced, of equal spring
from hand to top, and a casting line of suitable
weight, you will throw to the point you wish with
ease and softness—and walking upright, like the
"Lord of the Isles," disdain to crouch or hide. Thus,
too, by throwing out only half the length of line
you could do if necessary, you will in small streams

nip the trout up as he rises, and be more successful
by open means than by hidlins ; and why bind to
fish with one hand only* ?   If you have two hands
left from the Crimean or Indian wars, use both, except when you require to scratch your lug.   Thus
make your angling easy, pleasurable, and man-like.
The balance of rod should be thus—when you hold
it by the butt, in a horizontal position, it should not
droop in the top, though on the point of doing so ;
and it is an observable fact, that a well-balanced rod,
always feels one half lighter in the hand than an ill-
balanced one, although both of the same weight, upon
the whole, if weighed in scales.   This occurs from
being top-heavy, or too yielding in the middle, where
it should stand stiffest, yielding rather more both
below and above the centre.   I approve also of the
extreme top for two, or not exceeding three, inches
being very pliant, such as whalebone rendered finely
small will make it ; as in fishing on the stream-water,
say on a summer evening, when good sized trouts
are feeding on small flies, a stiff top will strike the
grip from their mouth as fast as you hook them ; than

* We have always found a one-hand rod the pleasantest to angle
with, because it fatigues less than a two-hand one. A light one-hand
fly-rod brings more trouts to the creel too, because the angler can
cast oftener with it than a two-hander, and the oftener the flies fall
on the water the more chance for trouts, of course.—[EDR.]

which nothing in all my experience in angling has
been more provoking, and which this thin, pliant, two
or three inches at the top will thoroughly prevent,
without making any observable difference in the
general spring of the rod.   It is also serviceable in
making a large trout, when hooked, keep down in
the water, and not spang and spatter on the surface,
beating the hook from his mouth;* and this (over
and above your necessary means in lowering the fore
part of your rod to near the surface) at a slanting
angle to right or left as may be, to keep him down
in the water till he get accustomed to be led tamely,
like a horse in breaking—tackle, after which he will
keep sleekly below, and come ashore resignedly.

This, recommended from our own practice, is upon
the whole more pleasant fishing than wading five or
seven hours even in boots, not to say in stockings,
and sometimes to middle waist in cold spring days,
or early summer weather, as I have often done,
labouring with a longer rod than here recommended,
to throw far out to where the trouts were resorting,
endeavouring to fill a basket with twenty-four pound
weight.   This you pursue with your limbs benumbed, till coming home, you require to be rubbed down
like a hunting horse an hour in your stall, or rather
before a fire, till you find the circulation beginning

to prinkle over your benumbed joints, when you again venture to conceive yourself safe from the seizure of rheumatism for a month or more to come. I have luckily escaped rheumatics to a long age, which to myself is a wonder, and matter of particular thankfulness, for what I have described is not rational treatment of our corpus.

ON THE DRESSING OF FLIES.

Despairing to give any practical idea by mere description of the manner of dressing flies, it might perhaps be as well to refrain from attempting it, as the methods of holding the flies while dressing, and the opinions as to where you should begin and finish are so various, agreeably with taste and habit, even amongst the best practitioners. For instance, my son and I laugh at each other's method of holding the salmon hook while dressing it, whilst we contend for the best finish—he holding it loosely in his hand, while I keep it linked to a hold-fast. Briefly then : tie on the gut, beginning at the head end of the hook, lapping it firmly along till nearly opposite the point of the hook, where tie down the end of the tinsel, and if a hackle is intended, there also tie the point of the hackle ; then dub the fur for the body on the waxed thread, and lap it solidly in a regular progression upwards to nearly the head end of the fly, and there fasten the thread till the tinsel is rolled forward, and the hackle beside it ; which of these is the first rolled on is of no consequence, providing the hackle is laid close in to the wake of the tinsel, to be as it were guarded by it from the teeth of the fish. When all is brought forward, and neatly fastened down by the tying thread, rather less than a quarter of an inch from the end of the shank, then add whatever bright tuft of colour you choose to put below the wing ; again fasten the thread, and pick all the body of the fly with a small awl or pin, and adjust it. Lastly, lay on and tie down the wings unbroken, crossing them with the tying thread as often as may be seen necessary to adjust and hold them fast, and then fasten your thread by a few knottings around the head of the fly.

Trout flies I dress the reverse way, beginning at the tail end of the fly to tie on the gut, lapping it up to within a little of the head, and putting the wings on first. When these are properly set and adjusted by the crossings of the thread, I choose my fur, and dub it on the thread, rolling it round for body, and fastening the thread. The fly is thus produced in a twinkling.

To dress trout flies in a superior style :—When the hook is tied to the gut and ready for the wings, cut with a pen-knife two wings close from the rib of the feather, lay the one piece upon your left fore finger, and the other exactly upon it, with the two insides together, then close your thumb upon them, and place the hook below, pressing it up close to the wings ; and while held in this position, lay the tying thread round over it, press the point of your finger closely on the tying thread, and while in the act of drawing tight, also cause it to draw the wings straight down together on the hook so as to prevent its ruffling or twisting them to one side ; then lap the thread once or twice more round on the same place to secure the wings, and letting the wings escape from your fingers, divide them asunder, and cross them round between with the tying thread, and they will stand up unruffled in the texture, a beautiful model of the living water fly.*

One may even go the length of cutting the two wings from the two corresponding feathers of the pair of wings from the same bird, but this is extreme

* John says truly, that to give any practical idea by mere description of the manner of dressing flies, is a difficult matter ; and though his description to a dresser may be pleasant and intelligible, to a novice it cannot be so. An angler will learn more in the art of dressing by a half hour's lesson from a regular hand than a half day's reading of clear English on the subject.—[EDR.]

nicety, which may only be resorted to as a trial of skill.

I may observe, however, that not above one of fifty to whom I have shewn this method of putting on the wings has ever succeeded in doing it well, but this I consider proceeds only from want of practice.

I have often thought that in the *trade* of fly dressing there is too much of show and variety, and tinsel-glitter, even for any river. Such flies I deprecate, and I suspect those who make them do so merely to increase their sale, as inexperienced anglers are apt to conceive that they ought to provide themselves with every variety of hook exhibited to them in a tackle shop.

As to the question of dressing salmon flies on whole length threads of gut, or on loops, I consider it merely a matter of taste or convenience, as they may be neatly and effectually done either way. Looped hooks are perbaps more convenient to pack and carry, and also require a less stock of gut on hand, either for the dresser or the purchaser. If looped, I would recommend the loop on small flies to be rather of three-ply twist of small fine gut than of one stout thread, as the three-ply is tougher, and it should be kept so short that the double eye may barely admit the single stout gut to which it becomes attached, after being opened by inserting the point of a pin, so that the last fastening running knot may form what may be considered a small head to the fly. For regular fishermen on the water, who generally dress or repair a fly or two every morning as their principal dependence for the day, perhaps the plain gut without a loop may be as well; it is as neat and efficient, and quite as convenient.

ON THE CASTING OR WHEEL LINES.

In either salmon or trout angling I do not like too light a casting line, as it does not throw so well, particularly in any breeze of wind. I prefer a casting line of three or four lengths of good horse hair, firmly twisted with the fingers (not plait), and not looped to take off and on the wheel line, but neatly lapped to it, so as to remain and be rolled up along with it. The first length of twisted hair should be nearly as thick as the wheel-line, suppose eight, ten, twelve, or fifteen horse hairs; the second length some two or three hairs smaller, and so on downwards, until about the fourth or fifth (according to the length of the hair), forming between five and six feet in all. Let the last be six, eight, ten, or twelve hairs thick, according to the strength of the hair, or the weight of the line wished, for salmon, trout, or both occasionally, as I generally have used them.* Then begin with three equal hairs of hand-twisted gut, choosing the hairs finer as you come downwards the four or five lengths, till, if for spring salmon fishing, the last is small enough to be next the hookgut, to which it should be attached by a neat loop. In clearer, summer weather, when single gut becomes necessary, have three or four additional lengths of good gut along with you, ready knotted and looped, to link on in addition to the former, which can be added or removed agreeably with circumstance or fancy. Let all the knots be well tied, both of hair and gut, and the ends neatly lapped down with waxed thread, so that you can roll all up through your rings without rag or hinderance; and when done with fishing, unlink the hook, and roll in all at once.

Wheel lines last best that are made entirely of

* We venture to state that very few anglers indeed would use the same wheel line for salmon and trout fishing, because to most anglers it would prove either too light for salmon or too heavy for trout. We do not know of anything more fatal to fine casting when trouting than a heavy bagging wheel line. It is as bad as a too stiff rod. The late James Baillie, the fly fisher, was very particular in this respect; and he could throw, with a rod cut from a hazel bush, the longest and finest line we ever saw fall on the water. The wheel line should be tapered as well as the hair and gut casting lines.—[EDR.]

horse hair, as silk, or a mixture of it, rots readily when wet. Even hair lines are not long in rotting if carelessly left wet on the wheel. If drawn off and hung up whenever they are wet, until dry, they will last very long, except the short piece of the end used in casting, which should be renewed frequently. I had a good wheel line, of my own making, that lasted me twenty-five years, fishing occasionally, both for salmon and trout, besides lending it often ; but I never suffered it to lie wet on the wheel.

A salmon wheel line for the Tweed here, at St Boswells, should not be shorter than at least seventy-two yards ; and all below Mertoun water about a hundred.

ON FISHING RODS.

[Very few anglers now-a-days think of making their fishing rods, and very few of those who do make them can produce rods to fish so well as those produced by regular makers. A good maker can adjust the spring and balance of rods to suit any angler. The woods now used by the best makers are : ash, sapling, or hickory for butt, and greenheart for middle and top, with sometimes a few inches of whalebone at the point. The best point we ever used was made of a bit of old brier, twelve inches in length, whittled into a taper and adjusted by James Baillie."—EDR.]

To produce the best fishing-rod for use and durability, take a billet of good hard red hickory, well seasoned (as it generally is before it reaches us here), of about three or four feet long, and have it ripped down into slips of various thickness, proper to form the whole rod, butt and top. Joint up as many pieces as will produce the length you wish, say eighteen or twenty feet long for a salmon rod, and from fourteen to sixteen for a good trout one. Make these into splice-joints of sufficient length, the splice being seven inches at least for the butt-joints, and tie them up well glued, leaving them so until the glue is dry; then lay the rod upon a straight plank, and have it planed up all in a piece to a proper thickness—a person of skill standing beside the joiner, trying and adjusting its elasticity to the proper spring, till he find it please, recollecting to allow something for the weight of the tyings of joints and rings. If the planing could be so managed, the perfection of the rod would consist in having it to taper properly the whole length, from butt to top, and the wood being of the same piece and growth, the *spring* must be equal and correct throughout. After it is properly planed and smoothly polished with sand paper, cut it across into two, three, or four pieces, as you please. Have your brass ferrules straight, not tapering, but alike wide at both ends and sunk just a little in the wood at the under ends, and left full and flush over the wood at the upper ends, and either with or without screws, according to pleasure.

These all adjusted, then roll up your wood-glued joints with good silk, or, what is preferable, very fine lint thread, using varnish on the thread rather than wax. Begin at the top to tie on the rings, which have large enough. Make them six inches apart at the top, and lengthen the distance between them as you come down towards the butt. Then have the whole slightly varnished.

If a rod is made up of various kinds of wood, or even of different trees of the same kind, you can never have the same equal degree of fine elasticity; whereas, by making the whole rod out of the same short piece, you not only improve the proper spring, but also find the best precaution against its twisting—to prevent which professional rod-makers often render the wood short and fragile by the application of heat, and other methods calculated to damage it in this most material respect. I prefer hickory, as it combines all the essential qualities, without the inconvenient weight of lancewood : only, great attention is necessary in selecting the hickory, as very much of it is unfit for rods.

To those who reside near the water, I would recommend a rod all of glued and tied joints,* as best

* Rods of this kind are in general use about Galashiels; and many anglers thereabouts uphold that these rods cast better than those made with ferrules. We used one of them for a season, a short one for fly fishing, and liked it.—[EDR.]

in point of real use, and not so liable to break in the moment of action : or, indeed, even for travelling, I would prefer tied joints, as, wherever a person has time to stop and fish, though only for a day or two, he has at least five minutes to spare for tying up his rod in a sufficient manner.

Rods are often breaking at brass joints, and those who use them, instead of bringing in a back-load of fish, are often arriving home from the water telling you, " I've broke my rod !"   Such sickening news may generally be prevented by tied joints.

A one-hand trout rod, between thirteen and fourteen feet long, is very convenient and pleasant to use, even when wading deep in the Tweed. But in moderate wading, we cannot command much water with a rod of less than fifteen or sixteen feet.   I would recommend that a rod be made soft and pliable for about three inches on the top, much more so than is generally done, as a hard springy maintop readily twitches the hook from the trout's mouth.

ON SALMON ANGLING.

The greatest requisite in an angler is the art of throwing his line properly. Though some attain this more easily and with less effort than others, yet it

is a point which can only be gained by practice, even
with the best rod; but when once learned, it is done
with little comparative exertion. And besides that,
in casting a good deal depends on a finely balanced
rod, yet as much depends on being accustomed to the
use of any particular one. I have seen a fisherman
in daily use of a rod so heavy and unyielding, that
any person else could hardly suppose it intended for
the purpose, and yet I have stood amazed at the
length of the line the owner would throw with it, from
the mere force of habit, whilst he in derision would
pronounce a fine soft springy rod " a mere wattle."
A stiff rod requires great force and quick motion in
bringing it back to give the requisite impetus to the
forward throw, while one of an opposite description of
make, from its tendency to yield, requires a very slow
motion to bring the long line fairly round with it
and communicate just the necessary quantum of force
to impel it again outward. Of course a medium is
best; and if we cannot possibly have a perfectly
equalized spring from hand to top (which, like per-
petual motion, it may be impossible to produce), then
let the stiffest part of the rod be about its middle, the
rest of it softening below and above to the extreme
top.

Practice with such a rod will make the best throw-

ing, and such a rod is also best for holding up the
fish in the *run*, without any tendency to jerk the hook
from his mouth on any sudden fling.

Indeed, the art of casting seems to depend on a
free motion of the body, and there seems to be a kind
of innate feeling, a delicacy of touch necessary to
throw a good line, which some may never be able to
acquire even by practice.   And though we have
known instances of gentlemen having killed salmon
on their first start out, when they could not throw
a good line, it has generally been under proper guid-
ance and direction on a favourable day, or on protected water, where fish were numerous and undis-
turbed, and "with all appliances and means to boot."
Such instances are, of course, no way indicative of
superior skill in the individual.

When the river is low and clear, then is the time
to prove the abilities of the angler.   Then a long line
is required; and great skill is shewn in making the
fly light like thistle-down within an inch of the spot
intended, say twenty-five or thirty yards from the
hand, and three or four at the least above and beyond
the spot where, from previous knowledge of the spot
or general skill, he knows for certain the fish must
lie.

I recommend a beginner to practice throwing the

line on a broad smooth pool, where he can see that it is delivered out properly, and falls lightly without splashing. In such case the practitioner will perceive something which he cannot easily account for: and that is, that after he has even attained a great degree of perfection in the art, he will not be able to distinguish how it happens, that in one throw his long line will proceed tightly out, his fly alighting first on the water, and in another throw the middle of his line will fall first, while the farther part, still obedient to the general impulse, will proceed out the full length, the fly falling the last on the surface. This last throw is not so good as the former, for the reason, that the main current having caught the middle of the line first, it carries it too quickly down, leaving the fly lagging and forming an awkward curve ; for, before it comes over above the fish, the fly should lie on the water, so as to have the appearance of plying at an angle against the current. And the angler should so manage his rod that, while he lets his line float round at its full length, his fly should come as slowly as possible over the main spot. In this case the salmon will sometimes rise at once, rather before you expect him, but more generally will follow the fly to the eddy, or edge of the deep, where, if on examination he feel disposed to seize the hook, he has it before you perceive a head, fin, or tail above the surface. Indeed, before you perceive the web of his tail he generally has the hook in his jaw a foot below water, as in descending he goes, like other divers, head foremost.

The angler's next motion is generally termed *striking*, which, to my taste, is a wrong word to express that particular action by which a true angler retains his already hooked fish. This motion is rather a retentive hold than a start, or a *strike*. Your tyro, keen and vigorous, is for ever *striking*, as the weakest part of his tackle, or a shred torn from the mouth of the fish will often abundantly testify; while the true angler will go through the whole process with perfect ease, or rather, in what an inexperienced onlooker would account a careless or slovenly manner; in short, as seemingly easy and unrestrained as the step and manner of the savage in his native forest,—so nearly do the accustomed habits of art approach the perfect ease of nature.

But I believe that in fishing, as in other things, example is more instructive than precept, and therefore a beginner would do well to set himself to observe with attention an experienced fisher begin and go over a stream or cast: his easy positions of body, method of casting, and manner of leading his line ; and above all, should he hook a fish, the way he manages him, until he is laid " broad upon his breathless side," a rich and beauteous prize. For instance, he will not *drag* his fly across the stream, neither *pull* it against the current, which is a common error with beginners, and quite absurd. But in salmon fishing, he will, in throwing his line, direct it so as to make the fly alight on the spot desired— not straight across the current, but slanting a little downwards, so that it may form as gentle a curve as possible ; he will move it as slowly as the current will permit, over the spot where he expects the fish to be lying ; he will make no perceptible motion to keep his fly on the surface, except on a sluggish pool, but will let it sink a little, depending on feeling rather than on sight ; and though apparently keeping no pull on his line, yet all the while he will be able to detect the touch of even a minnow. On a *boil*, or other appearance of a fish, he pulls up his line, not twitchingly, but actively, steps a yard or two back, rests a minute, to let the fish resume his lair and attention, and perhaps feels inclined to alter his fly to a shade darker, or a size smaller, before he annoy and disgust, or alarm his fish, when he will probably come up and seize it in earnest. Should he not rise again, or rise and pass it thrice,

8

leave him quietly alone for the present, and return
to try him some time afterwards. On taking the
fly, the fish means to return with it to his precise
select *spot* of lair, on rock, stone, or gravel, at the
bottom ; and the fine angler, holding him gently,
often in the first instance allows him to do so, but
soon the fish, too surely feeling his awkward predica-
ment, bolts off, "indignant of the guile." Then is
the time when the fisher is attentive. With the
butt end of his rod resting on his thigh or groin, he
keeps the top nearly erect, never allowing it to fall
below the proper angle of forty-five degrees, as relative to the situation of the fish ; and in this position
the elasticity of the rod never allows the line to
slacken in the least degree for a single instant, however the fish may shake, flounce, jerk, or plunge.
With two or three fingers and the thumb of his left
hand the angler holds his rod, while the wheel-line
runs out, regulated by the first, or first and second
fingers, relieved or assisted, as occasion may suggest,
by the right hand, when it can be spared from its
necessary occupation of rolling up the wheel-line, as
the fish settles a little or returns inwards. In this
manner the fish is allowed to run up, down, or across,
as he may choose. But if, when the fish makes an
outright dash of thirty or fifty yards aslant, ending

in a fling above water, the inexperienced angler
should feel flustered (which he is very likely to do)
and by some involuntary twitch of the running line
let the top of his rod be pulled down to a level with
his own head, then the tug of the last plunge will
assuredly break his hook or line, or tear the hook
from the mouth of the fish : or what is as bad, a
sudden jerk or turn of the fish will give the line a
momentary slackening, when the hold being already
so strained as to have widened, the hook will fall out,
and your fish is gone for ever.

More hooked fish are lost in these two ways than
from all other causes put together ; and this can be
easily prevented by a little self-possession, simply by
keeping up the top of your rod and letting the line
run with ease, regulated as above described by the
feeling of your fore finger.   But if the matter is properly managed the fierceness of the fish is the angler's
main sport.   The faster he dashes on, the sooner is
he exhausted.   Sometimes you may see him on the
opposite side of the river, with the web of his tail
above the water, and his nose struck into the gravel,
in an endeavour to dislodge the vile little instrument
of his ruin.   The fish will then again allow himself
to be led at ease to the angler's side of the river,
like a bridegroom to the altar, when, on finding the

water shallowing, he will again make another desperate effort, probably a new dash into the middle current; but, too much exhausted to resist the still continued pull upon him, he will soon again fall into the shallow, where, on a sight of his enemy, he is again alarmed into a new effort, and again exhausted by turning his outward-bound head down into the water again and again, and again, until his own last efforts to keep swimming are made subservient to the cautious angler, who moves him by degrees into the shallow, where, half dry, he must at last yield to his fate, and fall panting on his side. The angler should by this time have his line rolled up to within rod length, and the rod should be held with its top landwards, without slackening. The fish should then be seized with the fore finger and thumb of the right hand, across by the root of the tail (which is by far the surest method of seizure), lifted, or rather slid out head-foremost, over gravel and grass, and in mercy felled with a blow on the back of the neck.*

After going through this process with a twenty-two pounder (and the process would be the same

---

* The natives of Australia are said to drown the fish they catch by seizing them with the grip above mentioned, and holding them with the head below water. The gills then open, and let in the water, which drowns them in a minute.—*Younger.*

with a forty-four), the writer can aver, that he does not conceive that from the moment he has hooked such until he was laid on the grass, he ever, for an instant, had three ounces of more or less pull on the fish; for in all circumstances of run, regularity of pull is the sure test of true skill, and it leads to final success. Indeed, I have seen many a fine fish laid on the dry gravel, when the hold of the hook in the lip of his mouth was so slight as to be smaller than the steel of the hook : so much for equal pull and cautious management in the run. In short, a man is never a master angler so long as a desire to have his hooked fish to land excites in his feelings the least agitation, as the matter should be managed with that cool philosophical ease of mind, which is alike above the paltry calculations of loss and gain, and the common ridicule which often tends to stir up a degree of childish fretfulness. This perfect ease is absolutely necessary to first-rate excellence and ultimate success.

GENERAL OBSERVATIONS

ON

SALMON ANGLING.

The very perfection of the fly fishing art is to feel enabled to say, that you will take a salmon with fly, when, from the low clear state of the summer river, the regular fishermen, as well as the amateurs, have all given up the case as hopeless. To effect this you should take the smallest salmon fly, neatly dressed on a fine round thread of blue-clear, not white, gut. I dislike dyed gut; its natural colour, which I call *blue-clear*, is the colour of water, as may be seen by putting it into a white basin of water. The dark or blue colour of a river is the reflection of the sky, as seen on the surface from above. Such gut gives the same reflection when in the river. And what is still a better argument, the fish seem of my opinion, as they always take best with it.*

---

* When stating that gut in its natural colour is the colour of water, John was safe to add—"as may be seen by putting it into a *white* basin of water." If the white back-ground of John's basin could conveniently be held between the fish and the firmament, the gu t

As already said, for a low clear river take the smallest salmon fly ; and choose also the cloudiest or dullest hour of daylight, and *cast* in the manner formerly described over the deepest part of the stream or pool, where fish then lie, allowing your line and fly to sink deep in the water ; for though at this time the fish will not rise to a fly skimming on the surface, he will yet venture on a *bite* as it quietly passes near him below. In this way I have often succeeded to the admiration of even the fisher who rented the water ; and of late I have been delighted to hear a friend mention it as a point of his own discovery, and assure me he has often killed fish in the northern rivers, as well as in the ' Tweed, by following this plan, when not one *old*

under such a canopy would of course have little chance of being seen by the finny tribes. We have tried a number of experiments to find out how best to render gut invisible in the water, and we now decidedly prefer having it dyed (with logwood and copperas) of a blae or faint sky colour. Here are our reasons for preferring it : first, we have more difficulty ourselves in seeing it in the river than we have in seeing gut in its natural colour, and as *trouts*, at least, must often have it between them and the same back-ground—the river bottom and overhanging banks—we conclude that they will resemble ourselves in this respect. Next : the gut is *generally* between the fish and the sky when in the water, and being of a blue tinge, and seen against a blue sky, it must necessarily be more difficult of detection. Though dyed too, it remains transparent, as may be seen by holding it against the light. Gut in its natural colour may be almost invisible to the denizens of the deep on cloudy days ; but for successful and pleasant trout angling give us the "glad sunshine and the laughing sky."—[EDR.]

hand, who knew every pool and stream, could stir a fin, or be persuaded to attempt a trial.

My friend writes thus :—" In these small waters, or tributary streams which run into the large rivers, you may fish with great success with what is commonly called a sea-trout hook. In several small salmon waters in Argyleshire, and other island streams in the west, I have fished successfully with hooks of the above size, when I could not stir a fin with a common sized salmon hook. And it may not be generally known, that in these smaller waters, salmon, grilse, and sea trout, will take the fly greedily when the water is in such a state of foulness, that those who have only been accustomed to the Tweed, Tay, &c., would suppose it the next thing to madness to attempt trying a fly of any kind." I may remark here, that if my friend had thought of observing carefully, he must have found this would not happen in the *swell,* but in the *fall* of such flooded streams, when these fish, like natives in an inundated district, were thrown out of their usual spots of habitation, and were still moving about in an unsettled and shifting manner. In this way, salmon occasionally take the fly in large, though more particularly in smaller streams; as the sand and mud are gradually subsiding, the fish driven into the shallows ascend to the surface, the water being purer there, and thus take the fly on the same principle that trouts feed generally. But trouts will not take the natural flies in the rising swell of a river. When it has begun to fall they attack them greedily even in the white muddy water.*

In regard to the different kinds of salmon flies applicable to the different rivers, he further states a curious fact :—" In no two rivers that I know of," says he, " do they angle with flies which at all resemble each other in point of shape and character. In the Spey, Findhorn, and Ness, rivers not above thirty miles apart from each other, the style of their hooks is nearly as opposite as possible. In the Spey, common drake, or mallard wing, with yellow or orange body, and black hackle from the breast tuft of the heron, is one of their principal hooks ; and another, a hook dressed altogether from the heron—namely, a blue or slate-coloured wing with hackle to match. In the Findhorn, again, nothing but Irish flies, or imitations of them, seem to succeed. And in the Ness, the flies used are of a much more quiet and modest kind, somewhat resembling

* This remark as to trouts not taking natural flies when the river is rising, we can testify in favour of, having on many occasions put it to the proof, both by throwing the flies into the water and watching them, and by angling with them.—[EDR.]

those used in the Tweed in point of materials, but
not generally so large in size, and the form is shorter
and thicker.   In both the Spey and Findhorn the
hooks are much larger than for the Ness.

"I am not able to say how far one might be successful in any river with a common Tweed fly, only
varying its size and colour to the state of the river
at the time; I think the chances are that one might
kill fish in any river with them, just on the same
principle that in the Tweed many are successful
with the bright gaudy Irish flies, which are so opposite to the legitimate Tweed hooks.   But I do
not think this has ever been properly and fairly
tried, for one is apt to adopt the hook commonly
used on the river he goes to, without giving himself
the trouble to inquire into the cause for such a form
or style being adopted.   For myself, I have hooked
and landed good fish both in the Tay and Findhorn
with the common Tweed fly,* and I am sure they
would do also in the Spey; although I allow that I
would not have the same confidence in fishing with
any other than the common and well known hooks
for each respective river."

An old friend of mine, John Haliburton, formerly

---

* Tweed flies are not nearly so much used now for fishing the Tweed
as Irish flies.—[EDR.]

fisher on Dryburgh water here, and afterwards at Craigo'er on Mertoun water, who removed to a farm near Hamilton about fifteen years ago, once accompanied three or four gentlemen on a day's stroll to the Clyde, where, with his old *Tweed hooks* (exactly such as I hav described) he saved the credit of the party by personally killing the only five salmon seen that day. But then I have never seen any man who could excel Haliburton in laying a fly to the eye of a salmon ; and yet his is the only instance I have known of an angler becoming excellent who was not bred to it from boyhood ;* for John had never once thrown a rod at the time he took a lease of Dryburgh water, being then a labouring man, a husband, and a father. But then he was one of the few amongst the sons of men who could calculate on the nature of things as they are, without regard to fashion or general opinion. While in Craigo'er, in the year 1816, I knew him, in five days of one spring week, kill with y, with his own hand, ninety-nine salmon (mostly *foul fish* and *kelts* of course), and on one of the days he caught twenty-four, many of them about and above twenty pounds weight. But, except John

* With due deference to John we may state that we know a number of very good anglers who never caught either a trout or salmon in boyhood. Perseverance and observation might, in our opinion, make ten men out of twenty fair anglers.—[EDR.]

Thomson, once in Newstead, or the Kersses, the Purdies, and Johnstones, who, on the Tweed, could ever throw a line with Haliburton?

But not to multiply instances bearing on the point, I find, from my own experience, and that of others in whose skill and judgment I place full confidence, that the matter is resolvable into this general leading principle—that large or showy flies suit best in deep, dark, or drumly waters, and the finer modest shades of variation, such as I have here endeavoured to describe, are necessary to entice in the settled calm of summer pool and stream.

But it is seldom difficult to find arguments in support of exceptions to any general rule, and I am aware that in no instance could it ever be more easy than in the very limited selection of flies I have described; because almost every fisher prefers a particular style of hook, and I am quite aware an angler might fish successfully for a life-time, and yet never use a fly that could be proven to be an exact type of any one here described. At the same time, I am certain that unless some of my principle can be detected in his hook, his general success will be far from coming up to his wishes and expectations.

ON TROUT ANGLING.

In Trout Angling, the whole process, like the casting, is of a lighter character, in proportion to the
lighter implements used, and varies considerably from
the salmon principally in this respect, that, as the
trouts lie or swim about in more varied situations,
according to the state of water, sometimes in the
main streams, sometimes in the eddies, and in still
heavier waters on shallow gravel beds, the angler will
perceive that on spots where he might be successful
yesterday, not a trout will be found to-day ; for in
heavy flooded waters they fall into easier situations,
and as the water clears and lightens, again seek the
deep for food, pleasure, or security.

On the subsiding of a flood, great *takes* are often
made in eddies, where all the finny breed are driven
in shoals to quiet nooks, creeks, and cairns ; and
where the frothy scum of the agitated surface is seen
collected and wheeling in circling motion, great
slaughter may often be made by any one who can
simply throw a fly ten yards out before him.   This
happens after the fine fresh spring, and early summer
floodings, in March, April, and May, and sometimes

later, according to the wetness of a season ; but, of course, only on the first day of the ebbing flood.

Hence, throwing the line for trout does not require the same regularity of plan and manner as the casting for salmon, since it is often more necessary to throw aslant, upwards, or straight across, than downwards.   And, indeed, in trout angling generally, it is very improper to hang the fly on the stream, far more so to pull against it, as the natural fly never floats in that direction.

In fishing either stream or pool regularly over, cast the fly across, or slant it considerably upwards, and let it float down the current of its own accord till it come gradually full round, managing your rod so as all the while to keep the line and flies under such command, that should a trout touch the hook unseen below the water, you can detect him on the instant.   This action is simply a *tightening feel,* as the trout is generally previously hooked from the natural resistance of the floating line.   If he is not felt to be hooked, then it is necessary to pull full up and make another throw ; but never let the first pull in feeling for a trout be so decidedly forcible as to be called a *strike,** for it ought not to be done with

* Younger is against *striking,* yet the force he would allow to be used, above and elsewhere, appears quite strong enough for good and secure striking ; but anglers know that every one has faith in his

a third part of the force requisite to lift the line clear off the surface, as is necessary when making another throw. Indeed, in casting generally for either salmon or trout, the angler should never snatch his line quickly from the water, but give it first a gentle pull, and let the lifting it be a second and brisker action ; as a large trout, or sometimes a salmon, may be following the fly, and may readily, at that particular instant, be just seizing it; and if you lift it with foolish force, the fish is struck off from the gut in his

own method, if by it he can generally angle successfully. There are many points that successful anglers differ keenly upon, which, in our opinion, but simply and reasonably proves that there are more ways than one of capturing salmon or trout. To *strike*, as most anglers know, is to make a quick turn of *the wrist*—a sort of slight twitch—very like the movement made by the wrist when a person opens or shuts a lock quickly with a key. This movement causes the hook to give a slight but sudden jerk, which secures the fish. If properly managed the fish will not be struck off, because the wet line yields as well as the top of the rod to any gentle movement of this kind. The mode of *striking* we here describe must be understood to refer to trout angling. As regards striking, in salmon angling, many first-rate anglers do not strike when they feel the fish, but merely make a sudden steady hold ; while other equally good anglers strike, some of them firmly, the moment they feel the fish take. When learning salmon angling we had a "blowing up" more than once for not striking when a salmon happened to touch our hook and get off unscathed, and we have also repeatedly brought censure upon our unfortunate head *for* striking when a salmon rose and touched the fly, and disappeared as we struck. These unpleasant lectures (for it is something dreadful—and a little odd, perhaps —to lose a fish and "catch it" at the same time) we received from old experienced anglers, who simply differed in their mode of hooking a fish. Most anglers strike, we believe, when fishing with a very large hook.—[EDR.]

mouth. In low waters, I have in such a way caught many salmon with the trout fly, on which, at such times, they occasionally feed ; and therefore, in Tweed trouting, I have always used a wheel line long enough to secure any salmon accidentally so hooked.

The manner, too, of angling for trout, as a driver lashes stage-coach horses is ridiculous, as if a large trout were foolish enough to take a fly so offered. The angler is still more foolish to strike the fly from off the gut in a fish's mouth, and come home with a tale of sad mishap that a great salmon had broken his tackle. An amateur angler here last season came from the water with a sad complaint against a monstrous salmon that had robbed him of his bait hook and gut line; and what a weight he was to be sure! My son, who had happened to tie on the angler's hook in the morning, trouting a little next day with the same *roe* bait at the spot, caught a trout not half a pound weight with the identical hook stuck in its stomach, and the thread of gut hanging nine inches from its mouth.

But constant and successful trout angling in the Tweed, or other pretty large rivers, requires the fisher to trash himself rather unmercifully, as to secure general success, it is absolutely necessary often to wade deep and long to get to where the trouts may

be lying; for to stand on shore and see them tumbling up in the main current of broad pool or stream,
or on he opposite eddy, is of no avail to fill a large
basket; besides, he must wait with Job's patience,
and shift about, often for hours, till the time when
they are pleased to feed, which is various and uncer-
tain; and more particularly so in the Tweed than in
the smaller streams, according to the circumstances
already described.

When a lad, I have often fished patiently for three
hours without the appearance of a fin; and in the
two or three succeeding hours have filled my basket,
which held nineteen pounds' weight. This happens
often under circumstances to us unaccountable, but
frequently on a fine forenoon, when the natural flies
are floating down, and not a trout stirring; and after
a break of thunder, or a slight shower, sometimes of
hail, or even a fine breeze of wind, they will get all
into motion at once, and feed voraciously. Much
depends on the state of the atmosphere, of the influence of which we are yet ignorant.

But the perseverance necessary to general success
requires the angler to strive and labour diligently,
to wade in awkward situations in a kind of half-
floating way, to creep on the narrow ledge of a shelving
rock, under pendent tree and brier, and perhaps over

hanging dripping precipices, jutting and shivery—
such as the Dun-Hare-Crag, Hawkslee Scaur, the
whirlpooling Fatterdon-Pot, or the black drowning
Gibson's-hole below; to fish sometimes on his knees,
pulling in the hooked trout by the line in hand,
as in such unfrequented situations the large one-
pounders are not yet acquainted with the hook, and
are therefore keen and ready.

But these were the sports of greener years! The
slippery foot on the loosening stone, or the tremulous
grasp, with the deep below, is not the task for lusty
manhood, or the stiffening bones of age. If ever now,
once in a season, I do try the trouting, I must get
on more in the way the old trout feeds, rather lazily
and shyly.

It has a sobering effect, to feel the play of youthful
muscle torpescent! Yet, though, like a well-hooked
fish, we must succumb at last, there is still a certain
pleasure in the reminiscences of some of our early
starts in such pursuits.

It is now forty years since I, then a boy, so
poor as not to be master of a hook or a ha'penny,
sallied out to the small burn (which, at that time,
yet unrestrained, like myself, chose its own vagrant
way from Elliestown House to the Tweed, circling
through the low rushy leas, forming dimple, pool,

and ripple), and *gumped** out half a stone of speckled trouts, where my neighbours never suspected such a thing existed.

The poet is in error when he says—

> The trout within yon wimplin' burn
> Glides swift, a silver dart;
> And safe beneath the shady thorn,
> Defies the angler's art.

This the trout cannot do, for his clammy nose is ever protruded, and clear round eye ever on the alert for a fly or a worm, and well the angler knows where and how to drop the line into the pool before him. When a whale is not *safe* in the Polar Ocean, talk, forsooth, of a trout in a burn! O dear shade of Burns, the poetical portion of your earthly feelings might have been too fine for an angler, as well as that of your grand successor Byron, or perhaps it might not, for all the fascination of song. I grant you, however, that even I, when a hungry laddie have often enough got into these fits of extreme sensibility, returning the small trout to the stream —

> As piteous of his youth, and the short space
> He had enjoy'd the vital light of heaven.

And, indeed, I have often felt the full force of Byron's

---

* To *gump*—to capture trouts with the hands, beneath the banks and stones—generally done in burns and small waters.—[EDIT.]

satirical remark on anglers long before he wrote it;
ay, and occasionally got into such qualms of reluc-
tance, that I would suspend my angling pursuits, and
admire the trouts tumbling up in the streams, sup-
pressing the desire to cast a hook amongst the free-
booters.   And the same sympathies have at times
unfitted me for some necessary employments of life,
yes, even to the length of requiring an effort of my
strongest philosophy to bring me to prune a rose or
pluck a flower!   This was nursing the poetical tem-
perament to an unnecessary tenderness.   " No angler
can be a good man," says Byron ; yet, I believe
these sensitive gentlemen, the poets, could all eat
lamb, veal, and oysters, as heartily as trouts can snap
up lovely *innocent* flies, or gobble the small fry of
their own species with all the mischievous appetite
of cannibals.   And, alas ! the sensibilities of genius
give no sufficient guarantee for that consistency of
character which would justify us in bestowing the
designation of *a good man,* on any human being.

ANGLING WITH WORM FOR SALMON.

Angling with worm for salmon is practicable only when the river is very low and clear, and in all dry and frosty weather.

In January 1814, when the Tweed was frozen on both sides, leaving only about a fourth of its entire breadth still open in the middle, John Haliburton fished with the worm, walking on the ice (a lad attending him with a long gaff), when he made great slaughter, until the ice closed over. His greatest difficulty was to keep the freezing line running. Worm angling, however, can only be practised most successfully in the very lowest state of the river, after the fish have *set up*, as the fishers term it, and will not take a fly. In the summer season, the best fishing hours are very early in the morning, from daylight till the sun has become too bright, or in a day grey throughout.

The worm used in this angling is called the large *dew worm*, from its being found in the spring and summer nights among the dewy grass. They may be seen in a morning lying linked in couples all

along the pathway sides, or on old leas, where.
on the least disturbance or tread of foot, they sink
into their respective holes in an instant.   Fishers
generally gather them in candle light, stealing softly
along, and seizing them before they can escape.
When required in cold seasons of the year, they are
dug from the earth in certain places where found
in greatest plenty.   They are kept in moss for some
days previous to being used ; and if long kept require
to be fed with a little cream or sweet milk, and red
earth or brick dust.*

Anglers differ in their choice regarding the size of
the two hooks proper to be used for this sort of bait,
but those most generally preferred on the Tweed are
large sizes, Nos. 18, 19, or 20 of Adlington's—the
other Nos. 15 or 16.   As they require to be shorter
in the shank for this purpose than for the fly, it is
requisite to break a piece from the shank of each.
The larger one is tied to the end of the gut, the other
as much farther up on the gut as to allow its point
to be turned round to the shank of the first hook,

* The brick dust for worms, we should think, must now be an ex-
ploded notion.   It has no effect whatever on the colour of the worms.
It is too dry to be swallowed by them, and this is the only method
by which the clay could redden them ; and we know to our cost that
it destroys them if kept anything long amongst it.   The dust being too
dry for the worms, is the means of taking the sliminess too quickly
off, thereby causing, first numbness and then death.—[EDR.]

and a little of the shank of each should be left untied for the purpose of catching into the worms, and preventing them from slipping down from their proper positions. The first worm is then put on by inserting the hook at its head, and running it up over that hook altogether, then turning the uppermost hook round, and inserting it also at the same incision ; then run the worm up over this hook also till the tail of it is fairly above the bend of the hook, and the upper part on the line above. A second worm is taken, and the hook entered about its middle, running it up also to the second hook, which is entered at the same incision, and run round in the loose end of the worm, which covers it over the bend and point. The remainder of that worm is pressed up till it appear contracted and thickened on the short piece of gut intermediate between the two hooks ; then a third worm is taken and run on the first hook head foremost, leaving its tail to cover and project over the point. This is called a full and proper salmon bait. Some use only two large worms in the manner of the first and third, with half a worm, or a small whole one put on the second hook to cover its head and point.

A few large grains of shot, ready nicked half through, are kept by the fisherman very conveniently

in a quill for the purpose of adding an additional
sinker to his line, as the strength of a stream may
require, and from three or four to ten of them may
be used as considered necessary. They are easily
closed on the gut line by a little pressure of the teeth,
and may be opened with a knife, and taken off at
pleasure, according as the angler requires it to sink,
or move on in the various strength of still or rapid
water. These are put two or three together, or some
inches apart at pleasure, none within a foot, nor exceeding thirty inches from the hooks.*

Thus equipped the angler will commence at the
head of a stream or *cast*, and proceed downwards in
the very same manner as if fishing with the fly, taking
a full step between each throw. He will throw well
over the fish-lair, and let his line and bait travel
gradually round, just making as much motion as to
prevent it sinking and hanking at the bottom, and
always lifting it gently for the next throw, in case
the fish should seize it on the instant. But generally
the fish will follow it, and commence nibbling at the
bait, quitting and seizing it alternately. Sometimes
he will run off with it a few yards, then quit it,
return, and seize it again, all which time the angler

---

* Drilled shot, which some consider preferable, can be had of most
tackle makers for this purpose.—[EDR.]

will cautiously give way to his motions, which appear very capricious, allowing the line to follow him freely, yet never permitting him to be altogether unfelt.

Sometimes these motions will be continued for a considerable time, five or even ten minutes, when he will quit and leave it altogether. But more likely he will attempt to swallow the whole bait, which he generally at last succeeds in doing; and this motion is understood by the angler from the particular twitching the fish makes in gobbling it. The angler at last feels that he has it pretty fast, and by a sudden resistence fixes him, when he is then run and landed in the same manner as if hooked with fly.

Salmon are very voracious in regard to the worm bait. I have known two fishers, each of whom has, at periods more than twenty years apart, met with the self same occurrence in the very same place—the *Bayhill Cast*, at Dryburgh Chain Bridge. The fish took the bait, and was run sometime from near the head to the foot of the stream, when by some accident the line was broken, or cut on a rock, within a foot or two of his mouth, when the fisher coolly put on a new tackle and bait, went up and began again at the head of the *cast*, and exactly on the same spot, hooked him again with much less ceremony than at the first, as the fish seized it this last time with great eagerness, and was run and landed with the first bait, hooks, gut, worms and all, hanging in his throat.

When the water has fallen very low, in drought, the first trial of this worm bait is a searching thing for the river. I have asked Haliburton,—" John, are there many fish yet left in the water ?" "I cannot just say," he would reply, "as the water has fallen so low they have been *set up* to the fly for some time past; but I will inform you to-morrow night how many are in the *Caul-pool*, the *Broom-ends*, and *Back-brae*, as I mean to be on them very early in the morning with the worm, and every one you know must have a passing *pook* at the first bait." I went down to the *Caul-pool* once about five or six in the morning, after a conversation of this kind, and found that John had already eight lying on the gravel.

ANGLING WITH WORM FOR TROUT.

The worm preferred for trout bait in the Tweed is what is commonly called the black-headed small tailed worm. In manured and fat clay soils, this worm is found of gross habit and dark colour; and where the soil is light and sandy, is of a bright colour. On digging any earth in dry weather, it is found rolled together resembling a mulberry or a cherry. When got in this state, they may be fished with as soon as gathered; yet, in general, to have them in proper order, they ought to be kept some time before being used, a few days at least, amongst moss, and the moss occasionally changed. If kept over three weeks or a month, they require to be fed with a little cream or sweet milk, and brick dust or red clay,* but always replaced into moss a day or twobefore being used, which renders themclean and tough.

Although trout may be taken with worm in any state of water, yet the most proper time is in the very lowest and clearest state of the river, from the end of May to the end of July; and the best hours

---

* We have no faith in either sweet milk, brick dust, or red clay, as food or colouring matter for worms. Abundance of fresh moss (Scottice fog) will keep them fresh and clear for months ; but a few *drops* of water should now and then be sprinkled over it, and it should be frequently changed. The worms are always ready for angling with when kept in this way, and their natural colour, when scoured of the clay within them, is reddish. They should be kept in some very cool place, and the dead and sickly worms removed daily. We are in the habit of keeping them in a wooden box sunk in our garden, the box of course rainproof ; and we have on many occasions astonished our friends with a sight of many hundreds of worms all fresh and clean in the scorching July. Tackle-makers in large towns supply worms at reasonable rates, and the worms thus sold are generally in prime condition for angling with.—[EDR.]

of the twenty-four are from the first break of daylight to six or eight in the morning.   If the day is
what fishers term "a grey day," dull, with the sun
shaded, or a little breeze, they will continue to take
the whole day.   And although considerable success
may sometimes be had under the bright sun, which
often indicates a degree of frost in the atmosphere,
yet a day of alternate cloud and sunshine is considered the very worst that can occur.

The rod proper for worm requires to be a little
stiffer than that used for fly, and the casting line
within five or six feet of the hook should be of very
tight round gut, with the knots well lapped* down to
prevent catching the stones.   One grain of lead shot,
No. 3, should be fixed on the gut above the first
knot, or about eight inches from the hook.   No. 11
of Adlington's is often used, but No. 12, or even 13,
are better sizes.

Anglers differ in opinion about putting the worm
on the hook, but the best practice is to enter the
hook at the head of the worm, and run it down till
the worm is brought up all over it, and leaving the
tail of the worm to curl over the point, which should
always be kept covered, as the trout is so extremely

---

* For angling in clear water, no first-rate anglers of the present day
lap the line-knottings, either for worm or fly-fishing.—[EDR.]

suspicious that he will hardly take a worm where the hook's point is seen.

Thus equipped for a start in low pure water, the angler lets out a line only about the length of his rod, and entering at the foot of a stream, continues to wade upwards, throwing his line nearly straight up before him, or occasionally only a little to the side, as the run of water in regard to his position may require, or where from habit he believes that a trout may likely be lying on the watch for a floating worm. As his worm and line travel down towards him, he keeps a continued check upon it by a perfect management in raising the point of his rod, and on feeling the least stop, he can generally determine whether it is a small or a large trout, the small one continuing to follow and nibble, while on the seizure of a large one the worm is stopped at once, when the angler gives a gentle pull, which being downward, against the trout, generally gets a secure hold of him.

In this way great slaughter is made of the very best trout; and this by a dexterous hand is accounted the most masterly mode of all trout fishing.

As it is necessary in very clear water to keep out of view of the fish, coming from below and fishing upwards in this manner gives the angler decided advantage.

By a skilful and diligent fisher, in our smaller rivers, trout may be taken with worm all the autumn in almost any state of the river ; and as in the colder part of the season trout generally leave the streams, seeking the more easy current of the pools. they will there also take a worm dropt near them ; in which case it is necessary to give the worm as much of a nice motion by the management of the rod, as to prevent it sinking and settling at the bottom.   One man I see daily (an old gamekeeper, in present lack of other occupation, and who "maun do something for his bread") is so excellent at this method, that he kills on an average about half a stone every day, in the Ale water ; and to-day (September 16, 1839), after yesterday's very high flood, while Ale water is yet white and muddy, he has come in with nine pound weight of beautiful trout, taken there with the worm. For harvest wages—half-a-crown-a-day and victuals —I dare say he could teach any active man to do the same in the course of a fortnight's diligent apprenticeship.

So far as regards fishing with worm in drumly or flooded waters, except by a knowing and dexterous angler, as above alluded to, I consider it merely a boy's amusement, generally done without art, and it is not worth further description.

In the Teviot, and all the streams between that and the Cheviot range of hills, particularly in the pastoral districts, where the Oxnam, the Kale, and Coquet waters glide through amongst sheep farms, great execution is done with a red and bright yellow freckled worm, called the *Brandling*, or Bramble Worm.* This worm is found in very old dung heaps and when taken out emits a strong smell, felt at a considerable distance. I have heard it affirmed that my grandfather, in the olden time, killed thirty-six dozen of trout in one day, in the Kale water, with that worm. I believe this the more readily, as I know that a nephew of mine killed half that number in one day with the fly, in that small stream. And a Jedburgh amateur angler assured me to-day, that

---

* The Brandling is still held in great repute, but not so much by clear-water anglers, as by those who angle when the water is subsiding after a flood. In pools the trout seem to gather about the sides wherein this worm is being angled with in the manner they do when roe is used. We met an angler of our acquaintance some years ago with a large number of trouts taken with the Brandling, all from one large pool, which was slightly muddy. On a bit of string he had twelve trouts that weighed 12 lbs. On another string he had nearly as much weight, though the trouts were rather smaller, and he had also a small gamebag full of the smallest he had taken, probably in weight about 8 lbs. The Jed was the river in which the *take* was made, and the angler's remark to us was that he believed he hadn't left a decent sized trout in the pool. His rod and tackle were of the coarsest description. He at one time fished so much with this bait, that he kept his supply of *seasoning* worms in a pretty large barrel. When a boy we on one or two occasions had a peep at the "barrel o' worms."—[EDR.]

he once killed the same number, eighteen dozen, in one day, with the Bramble Worm, in the Teviot.

Yet though these worms have been brought and bred here in dung, I have never known much success with them, nor heard that they were at all to be preferred to the common worm in Tweed fishing.

\

FISHING WITH MINNOW.

Minnow is a very good bait for either salmon or trout, although a very small trout or par, put upon the hooks whole, in the manner of a minnow, is a preferable bait for salmon. For trout the minnow may be fished with in any state of water, flooded or clear. It is best, however, in the evening, particularly in the shallow of a ford or the break of a stream. Some use three, four, or five hooks on the minnow bait, and put it on various ways; but the best practice is with two hooks, the largest, No. 14, the other, No. 8 or 9;* these are tied distant from each other the full length of the minnow. The large hook is entered at the mouth of the minnow, and

---

* The upper hook (the *lip-hook*) should be so formed as to keep the lips of the minnow close, to prevent its becoming destroyed. Tackle makers have hooks for the purpose.—[EDR.]

brought out at the root of its tail. The small one serves principally to hook its mouth and hold it on ; or the minnow may be reversed, with the same chance of success the large hook entered at its tail and brought out at its mouth, and the small one hooked through the gristly part at the root of its tail. As many lead shot are put on the line, a foot or two above the minnow, as will make it keep half sunk in travelling. Swivels are also necessary on the line, to prevent it twisting, although what is called "spinning the minnow" intentionally, is nonsense. It is just thrown in nearly straight across, and allowed to travel slowly round, like the salmon worm-bait, in about mid-depth of water, with only as much movement of the rod as to prevent it sinking and catching at the bottom. The trout seizes it sometimes with a dash, but more generally follows it slyly, and snaps it, getting himself hooked before the angler actually perceives him, which renders any idea of striking him absolutely ridiculous. The natural retention of the hand in fishing is generally sufficient to fix the hook in any fish without intentionally striking ; and in all angling it is proper to depend more on feeling than on sight.* For salmon,

* In angling with fly for trout, especially in clear water, we consider sight of much more importance than feeling. The expertest fly anglers we know "hook" the trouts as they see them rise.—[EDR.]

10

the principal minnow hook should be a size or two larger, say No. 15 or 16. And in fishing with this bait purposely for salmon, you go over the salmon cast with it just the same as with the worm or the fly, hanging it as long as possible, with a gentle motion, over the spot where you suppose him to be lying. But, as formerly mentioned, a whole small par, or young trout, is a preferable bait for the salmon. Sprats, or garvies, as they are called, which I believe are young herrings, are excellent bait for salmon. The first time they were tried in the Tweed was in the spring of 1837, at the first breaking up of the river, at which time I accidentally saw these sprats, and conceiving they would be good salmon bait, procured a few, and recommended them to a Mr. George Brown, then here on a fishing excursion. On his first trial with them he made great havoc amongst the salmon in Dryburgh water. He then took a few to Kelso, and there introduced them, where they became a favourite bait for the season, till, at last, the fishermen prohibited their use, from a supposition, that the daily use of such a large bright bait scared the fish from their waters.

PAR-TAIL

Par-tail is seldom used for salmon, but is a capital bait for trout. Two hooks are also necessary for this, the same as for the minnow, only of a larger size. No. 15 or 16 is small enough for the end one, the upper one No. 9 or 10. Measuring from the bend of the hooks, they should be tied about two inches and three-quarters apart, or a little more than half the length of the whole par, or trout, to be cut and used for the bait. Half an inch of the large hook should be left out untied, for the purpose of being run back and fixing the bait, to counteract its tendency to slip off. Any very small trout, par, or smolt, may of course be put on whole in the manner of a minnow ; but when too large for this, it should be cut across to the proper length, to suit the distance of the tied hooks, slanting the cut from above the back fin to a little below the middle of the belly. The fins and web of the tail should then be nearly all cut off, and the large hook inserted a little above the tail, and brought out at the cut end, leaving it to hang freely and clearly out. The other hook is put through the solid gristly part, above the root of the tail. The hooks thus left out have a fair chance to get hold when a trout bites. Swivels are necessary on this, as on minnow tackle, also shot to make it sink half-depth in rough water; and thus prepared, it is fished with the same way as the minnow.

Though trout will take the par-tail occasionally in any state of water, exactly as they do the minnow, yet the best time for using it is on the first swell of a flooded muddy river, and then best in the shallow, just above, or on the break of a stream. In this case I prefer using drag hooks—that is two hooks, No. 9 or 10, tied back to back on a strong gut, attached to the line an inch or two above the other hooks, and projecting three or four inches out beyond all. The first trial I made of this was when I was one day obliged to give up fly-fishing by a sudden flooding of the water from a thunder shower. This was exactly on the spot where the Merton Bridge is at present founded. Of a dozen good trouts then caught in a few minutes, eight were hooked outside the body by these trail hooks. I have consequently preferred them ever since in coloured water, and with them have been always proportionally successful.

In minnow and par-tail fishing, however, one cannot succeed well every day on the same spots of water : the reason is quite obvious.

Minnow and par-tail are excellent baits in the night throughout the summer, in all states of water. But night fishing cannot be recommended; it is so baneful to the health.

Minnow, for *bait*,* are caught various ways, with nets or with worms; but boys will always provide them for a trifle. And the moment they are caught they should be dropt in a box overhead amongst salt, for preservation, unless they are to be used that same day.

ROE BAIT.

[By Act of Parliament, angling with roe is now prohibited, but we deem it proper to let the following chapter stand, as it records the method by which trout were captured by it; and besides, Acts on fishing are changed almost annually. Roe-fishing in muddy water, in autumn and winter, we always considered should have been beneath the notice of proper sportsmen: to capture trout in such water requires no skill, and the fish in such seasons are thoroughly out of condition. In summer floods, however, when trouts are in their prime, sometimes heavy baskets used to be made by roe-bait. —EDR.]

Salmon roe has, of late years, become so fashionable as a trout bait for all seasons of the year, that those who profess superior methods of preparing it have generally a demand above their means of supply.

* Small minnows for trout angling are best, and they should be white-bellied. The reddish minnows, commonly called "streamers" are not taken readily by the trouts.—[EDR.]

After all, I must confess I have never seen much
success with it, except on the first of the autumn
or winter floods, when, for a day or two in the subsiding river it is most deadly.

One thing that particularly recommends this bait
to so many is the simple method of its application,
being level to any capacity.

Receipts for preparing the roe are held as secrets
by individuals; but the object of all and each is to
preserve it clean, and near the natural colour. Some
prefer it broken into paste; others preserve it as
whole in the roe as possible. One receipt I can here
give:—Take the roe from the belly of the fish, and
put it in water, a little more than milk warm; stir
and wash it till the roe leaves the netting and runs
like shot; clear away the refuse, then drain it, and
hang it in a flannel cloth to drip, for twelve hours or
more; put it then in a vessel, and salt it, adding a
small quantity of saltpetre, and set it in the open air
to dry, or before a fire, not too near; then pack it
in small pots, and run a little suet over it, to exclude
the air, when it will keep for years. But at the
same time, I must confess, that the best success I
have ever seen with the roe bait has been with it
simply salted as taken from the salmon's belly, even
unbroken from the netting, laid on a board or slate,

set in a sloping position, to let the blood and wet run from it while absorbing the salt. When half-dry it is best for use; but if long kept, till dried hard, it should be dipt in water, to soften it a little before being used.

The hook used is No. 9, 10, or 11, just tied on the gut like any other bait hook. The only great error in this fishing is using too large a bait; the size of a pea of prepared roe is always sufficient; any larger piece prevents the hook from catching, in which case the hook is pulled from the trout, generally leaving the bait in his mouth.

The proper places to angle are on the eddies of strong or flooded water, on some fine gravelly bottom, where the trout have come in shoals to the quiet water ; and there it is only necessary to drop in the bait, and wait till a trout is felt or seen to move the top of the rod ; then pull up, lead it out, and throw in again for another.

The best time is the morning. I have seen a lad bringing in at breakfast time seven dozen, which would weigh above two stones ; and a boy lay down beside them half the number, which would over-weigh one stone; and these had been caught with the plain roe, simply as salted from the belly of the salmon.

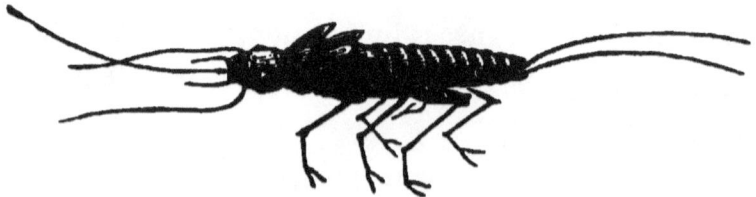

CREEPER FISHING.

BY THE EDITOR.

Its head was covered wi' a black airn ladle,
It had black legs, and tail as sharp's a needle,
A great red e'e stood stairin' in its breast,
I'm like to swarf—O, 'twas a fearfu' beast !—

Tannahill.

Though the creeper has long been known as a deadly bait to the knowing ones who have used it, so conservative are anglers in general, that it is only within the last year or two it has been much used on the Borders, especially on the lower parts of the Tweed, and on the Teviot and its tributaries. Younger himself was influenced by this feeling, and said he "couldna be fashed to write aboot it; it was sic a short time on." Cotton knew it, and calls it a Jack, the name, by the way, of a fish common in the

English rivers. He never mentions it as a bait; but he knew it as a deadly one in its winged state, and says that the fishes " will gorge themselves with those flies till they purge again out of their gills." Hawkins, writing a hundred years later than either, had never seen it, while his " learned and ingenious friend " knew it as a stone-fly, but not as a creeper. So far as we are aware no books on angling treat of it as a bait but those published in the present century. Barker is known in angling history as the first who found " following the roe" a successful expedient for filling the creel; Smail as the first who found the minnow to be a salmon bait; but the name of the originator of creeper-fishing must have been "written upon water."

The creeper is not such a short time " on " as the trusty John imagined. The insects are in the river all the year round. We have seen them in almost every month of the year, and of all sizes, from an eighth part of an inch in length to the full-grown insect. But it must not be imagined that the season for angling with the creeper extends over such a period. In general we have found it a good bait from about the middle of April to the middle of June, when it merges into the stone-fly. One of the largest *takes* we ever made with it was on the

20th of the latter of these months. Stone-flies were in abundance at the time, and we tried both these and the creeper carefully for an hour or two, but finding the latter by far the deadliest of the two, we stuck by it to the end of the day. We have tried the same baits in a like manner several times since with the same result; but of this more hereafter.

"Up in the morning early" must be the angler who would be successful with the creeper at the beginning of the season; for, frosty or fresh, it is then most deadly before the first glimmer of the sun strikes the water; only that is generally an hour or two after sunrise. After the sun is up a fair number of trouts may be taken down to about 9 or 10 a.m., when the artificial fly is preferable. By the beginning of May, however, a change in this respect gradually begins to establish itself, until, by mid-May a total reverse has taken place. From that period until the end of the season, the best time for creeper-fishing is from about 9 a.m. to 5 p.m. For success, however, the water must be low and clear, otherwise the creeper will prove useless. A two-inch swell, though the water remain quite clear, will cause the trouts to stop taking it; and this we have found to be the case over and over again, both in the Tweed and

elsewhere. Under a brilliant, steady, June sunshine
—a great fishing help—by a low clear water, with
a dozen or two of creepers, and cunning in the fling
of his arm, he is but a sorry angler who does not for
the time forget friends, home, and country.

The creeper is fished with in the same way as
worm, by throwing up-stream ; but in place of fishing
the comparatively smooth streams that worm is used
upon in April and the beginning of May, the creeper
during that period should be fished in, or rather upon
the edge of, very rough water. The best conditioned
trouts only can lie in such water at that early season,
and in general, only the best conditioned trouts take
it,—a consideration. Indeed, at such a time, we do
not recollect ever capturing more than two or three,
or so, in any other than pretty rough water. Where-
ever an eddy is brushed by a strong and moderately
deep stream—a place where good trouts, if they are
in the water, are sure to be lying—the creeper should
be applied, and, if possible, dropped just between the
eddy and the stream. All broken water where trouts
lie, such as that below mill caulds, and large stones,
is favourable for creeper-fishing, especially during
the first few weeks after the insect comes in as a
lure. When the trouts begin to take it freely
through the day, however, the sport becomes more

pleasant; as in all the common feeding-streams, rough
or rippling, but especially in those streams with
pebbly margins—the haunts of the insect—the lightly
thrown creeper will prove a surer *giant*-killer than
Cotton's "most deadly killing fly," of which he sings.
When May has given place to June, and

> " When the sun gallopes in his full career,
> And gildes the streames with heavenly Alchimy,"

the finest and thinnest streams covering good trouts
may be fished with success. By now and then casting to the very edge of the water, large trouts at
times may be captured, as they prowl about the
edges of the pebbled streams on the look out for
vagrant creepers and water-worms. We know that
they poach in such places, and remove the fences
that protect these unfortunate little animals. We
and others of our acquaintance, have several times
seen trouts—especially so when the rivers were very
small from drought—turn over pebbles with their
noses; and but for the food they procure in this
manner, when the rivers are low, we do not see how,
when taken, they could so often have large numbers
of creepers and water-worms in their maws, and also
such large quantities of water grubs, which are well
known to lie beneath the stones. The water-worms

(a species of the earth-worm, with black heads and reddish bodies) we do not recollect ever seeing, though they are numerous, either in the water, or at the edge of it, unless we turned up the stones under which they were lying.

In a very bright June day—if a curl on the water all the better—a few good trouts may be captured in still-water by throwing the creeper into the edges of overhanging banks; and large trouts may also be taken in water just gathering itself to form a stream, or in other words the *hing* of the stream, which every angler knows who can pronounce Auchtermuchty. We would not, however, advise the angler to dwell long on such places, as the streams are certainly the preferable parts for sport. Nor should he dwell long on one stream if he have another unfished above him. It is not good policy to cast half-a-dozen times over the same trout, or even twice, when trouts are lying a step further up that may not have had a line over them for an hour or two, and may therefore not be so wary.

In all kinds of clear-water fishing, it is almost needless to say that very fine stained gut should be used. No doubt, in the early part of the season, when the trouts are somewhat *green*, gut of a heavier stamp may be angled with; but, for our part, we

prefer fine gut at all times, unless in muddy water.
We may mention that horse-tail hair is a very good
substitute for fine gut when the latter cannot be had.
This is like taking a step backward, because gut
superseded hair; but now that much difficulty is
often experienced in procuring proper gut, the angler
will find hair both easily got and a capital substitute.
We often use it ourselves, and always single, and we
find no difficulty in landing trouts with it, saving
that it takes more time to land large trouts, and as
a whole, a little more caution when *striking* and *landing* than gut. Hair when wet is very elastic, so that
a trout making a sudden bolt is not apt to break it;
and if it be good hair trouts up to about half-a-pound
may be lifted out of the water with it. If of a blae
colour, it is also nearly invisible in the water. Hair
from the tails of white or grey nags is best, *horse-
hair* being generally too coarse, and that of mares
too brittle. When we have gut to our taste, however,
we prefer it. It is more clever among *taking* trouts.

Some anglers, rather innocent ones we opine, make
up their lines of any sort of gut, and bait the creeper
upon a common worm hook—passing it through immediately below the head, and then back again
through the head's antipodes. This is a vague
way of making a line, and a clumsy style of baiting;

and shows moreover like the hidalgo's dinner—very little meat and great deal of table cloth. The general mode of baiting the creeper is on two hooks of size about No. 4 Addlington, which are tied about half-an-inch or so apart. The upper hook, which some anglers prefer a size smaller, is passed sideways through the shoulders, and the other in the same way through the lower part of the body—rather lower than the middle. Though many first-rate anglers use the two hooks, we cannot say we have a liking for that style of baiting the creeper. We consider that two hooks cannot be sufficiently hidden in the body of such a small bait. We use only one, a No. 5 Addlington sneck-bend, the point of which we enter (*see illustration*) just above the breast bone, and carry down the inside of the body, and bring out at the belly, immediately below where the legs protrude, taking care not to bring out any of the *interior* of the insect. The hook, besides being fixed in the strongest part of the insect, is thus almost hidden—the tip of the shank being almost flush with the nose of it, and the point protruding from the bend only; and by baiting in this style the creeper is made to come down the stream on its back, and the protruding hook-point is thus rendered invisible to the trout. The hook itself is a keen one, and very few trouts are lost by it if they once take hold. The best angler who ever thrashed water—James Baillie of Lauder—baited the creeper in exactly the opposite manner to that we ourselves practice. He, knowing that trouts sieze all live provender by the head, inserted the hook below the legs and brought out the point above the breast bone; but the insect when baited in this way is apt to slip round the bend of the hook after the first cast or two is made; it is also more difficult to bait it so without injuring it.

Great care must be taken in casting with the creeper, otherwise it gets destroyed: and those who find that they cannot make a cast sufficiently soft for the preservation of it, should use the two small hooks just mentioned, as they keep it in better preservation; moreover, the two small hooks have been the means of filling many a capacious creel. As the creeper is soft and easily destroyed, it is difficult to throw a long line; so that to keep out of sight the angler must stoop at certain places. Should he turn *creeper* himself here and there he may find it profitable. When fishing with this bait we almost never use a sinker, as the trouts rise and take it about mid-depth, and often within an inch or two of the surface, even in heavy streams. In very heavy streams, however, a single shot, No. 3 or 4, may sometimes be used advantageously. Without a sinker there is little danger of the hook getting fast on stones or the like; and when the angler sees his line stop, he should *strike* almost on the instant.

We have many a time been amused with the timidity shown by anglers, even anglers, when they took a creeper in their hands for the first time. The poor animal is generally thrown to the ground as if it were a live coal, and often with a profane ejaculation accompanying it. It certainly is not a pretty animal, and its nimble legs tickle the palm of the hand; but the angler soon gets over his timidity when he finds the reptile-looking innocent a deadly trout-bait.

The stones, large and small, under which creepers are to be found, are embedded loosely among clean and generally pretty coarse sand; and where the insects lie the water is always *running*, and that, from one inch to five or six inches deep; and when the river gets less as the season advances, they retire with the river, but still keep under stones of a similar kind. Places abounding with stones and sand, as described, are in rivers generally plentiful; and in such places, in a dry spring season, no difficulty need be experienced in procuring abundance of creepers. When taken, they should be kept in a perforated tin box, dry

11

and airy, and in this way they may be kept living for some days. A number of anglers gather what serves them when fishing, but we prefer having a goodly number to begin with; and we use only the largest-sized when we have them to pick and choose from. In a wet spring, sad to relate, when the rivers keep swollen, the sport from creeper-fishing proves a dead letter; and at the end of such a season the disconsolate angler may sorrowfully exclaim:

They lived unknown, and few could know
    When creepers ceased to be:
But they are in their grave, and oh,
    The difference to me!

Mostly all the streaming rivers running over loose gravel beds are adapted for creeper-fishing; such as the Tweed, the Leithen, the Gala, the Leader, the Rule, and the Teviot, the latter being better for this kind of fishing above Roxburgh than below. Trout taken with creeper in the Gala and the Leader are of a heavier average than those taken in the same rivers by worm or fly when the water is clear, and we have found the same result in the Tweed. To give an idea of the size of trout taken in the Tweed with creeper, we way mention the weights of some we captured in 1859 in that river. Out of twenty-seven trout

captured in an April morning, the best half-dozen
weighed 5 pounds. In another morning in May,
out of twenty-one trout, the best half-dozen weighed
5½ pounds. On a bright afternoon in June, also in
the same year, we went out for the purpose of fishing
a single favourite stream. There were half-a-dozen
anglers on the stream when we began, and we only
got eight trout, but these weighed 6 pounds; and
on a May morning in 1861 we killed a dozen, the
best half-dozen of which weighed 6½ pounds. In
Leader Water, in June 1863, we caught three dozen
and nine, which weighed 14 pounds. The largest
trout we ever killed was with creeper, and it weighed
3¼ pounds. Indeed, we do not know of a bait,
except the minnow in flooded water, that can fill a
creel with larger trout than this insect; and those
who angle with it know that they are but little
troubled with the small trout and fry that sometimes almost pester a man's existence out of him
when using the artificial fly.

THE STONE-FLY.

[OR BORDER "MAY-FLEE."]

BY THE EDITOR.

I am the daughter of earth and water,
And the nursling of the sky.

Shelley.

STONE-FLIES come into existence—we mean numerously so—generally about the second week of June, and continue a good bait for about three weeks or little more. We have found clusters of flies, however, beneath large stones in the end of March. They are found under the dry stones at the side of the water wherein they live in creeperhood. For a day or two after merging into stone-flies they are tender and somewhat helpless, and many of them perish when exposed to cold east winds. Great numbers, too, are blown into the river before their time when the weather is windy—their wings being so large that they act like sails, and drive the insects in all directions in such weather. The flies are therefore most plentiful in mild seasons; but in all seasons they are most numerously to be gathered in places where the banks of the river shelter them from the wind. But a single flood, if high and of long duration, will sometimes sweep off the whole flies of a season.

When the river is *falling in*, and is of a porter colour, it is in first-rate trim for fishing with the stone-fly; and the streams and eddies are the best places to fish with it; but a number of trout may at same time be taken with it in the pools. When the water is clear the only places worth fishing with it are rough streams, and in such places it is sometimes very deadly. In swollen rivers of the porter colour above mentioned some of the largest *takes* have been made with stone-fly that ever were made in the south of Scotland; but it very seldom happens that the porter-coloured river and an abundance of stone-flies are to be met with in a state of co-existence. The trout taken with this bait are large and of the best quality—better on the table than those taken with worm during the same season. Indeed, we never saw a trout taken with it in any other than good condition.

The stone-fly must be fished up-stream, like the creeper, and it is baited in the same way; and only the large yellow-bellied flies, the females, should be used, if they can be had, as they are much more deadly than the little black-bodied males. Some writers on angling recommend fishing with two of the

male flies on the same hook on account of their small-
ness. This we have tried often, but never with anything like success; we therefore prefer using one fly
at a time, however small. A successful stone-fly
angler of our acquaintance, who has used it as a bait
for more then thirty years, is also against using
two of the male flies at a time in place of one.

As the fly is more easily destroyed and jerked off
the hook than the creeper, a shorter line should be
used, which should be thrown very gently out; and
common sense will, of course, tell any angler that
no sinker should ever be used with it. When thrown
into streams, the tumbling· of the waters generally
takes the fly under the surface, and we have mostly
found it more readily taken when so placed, than
when floating on the surface, especially so in slightly
muddy water. In pools, however, we prefer having
it floating; and in these the stone-fly is generally
most deadly about nightfall. Quick *striking* is
necessary when angling with this bait.

We mentioned in our remarks on creeper-fishing,
that from experience we found the creeper more
deadly than the stone-fly when both were co-existent.
This, of course, was in clear water; the stone-fly
being as deadly, if not more deadly, in swollen or
coloured water, as the creeper is in clear. Here is

a method we have found successful when both in-sects were to be had : we used the creeper on ordinary and thin streams, and when we came to very heavy water, where a shot might probably have been needed on the creeper-line, we used the stone-fly.

Lord, what a stoun'! a glorious stoun';
My saul played dirl against my croon,
My feet near loupit frae my shoon
    When first I heuk'd a saumon.

But dearly tho' sic sport I prize,
Wi' eager heart I aften rise
As dawn lichts up the simmer skies
    To fish, an' *no* for saumon.

For whiles I dance wi' vera glee,
When, wi' the deadly bait or flee,
The mornin' brings some *troot* to me
    As big as mony a saumon.

An' when the troots are takin' fine,
The deil might try to clutch my line,
The sun an' mune forget to shine—
    I'd trail them oot, like saumon.

REMARKS ON

WORMS AND WORM ANGLING.

BY THE EDITOR.

LAIRD (*bawling across stream*)—What are you doing there, Jock?

JOCK (*with difficulty*)—Fiffin!

LAIRD—Fiffin? Oh, fishing you mean. And what's that in your mouth?

JOCK—Wo'ms fo' bait.

LAIRD—O, you brute!

JOCK—Weel, I might as weel have carried the brutes in a flannen bag, maybe. *Jest Book*, 1760.

WE have successfully practised worm-fishing—the surest of all fishing—in clear water for many years, and as our ideas on the subject differ somewhat from those of Younger, who does not appear to have angled much with worm, we shall herein note some of our experience: merely premising that on a subject of this kind the tyro may find the experience of two anglers of more benefit than one.

Worm-fishing generally may be practised most successfully from about mid-May to the end of July.

Trout in good condition may however be captured earlier or later in the season, according to the piscatorial "earliness" or "lateness" of the respective rivers. For instance, the Till and the Eden are early rivers, and the Rule and the Oxnam are late. Burns and upland streams in general are late, and may be angled in successfully after worm-fishing is almost over in such waters as Tweed and Teviot.

From the middle of May till about the middle of June, the early morning and forenoon is the best time for worm-angling; and from that period—but the change of course takes place by degrees—the best time to the end of July is from seven, eight, or nine o'clock, till about four or five in the afternoon.

From mid-May to mid-June the trouts take worm greedily on very fresh or dull mornings, or when very light rain is falling; and in the sunshine of early June they also take greedily. But they are not constantly in taking humour, and the angler must cultivate patience if he wish to make a good basket. Trout often do not take, as Younger says, at a time when even first-rate anglers think, from all outward signs, they should be feeding; but a good angler bides his time, knowing that they must have their "grub," and that is perhaps one of the reasons why good anglers can always bring home a weighty dish, if not a basketful, after a day's sport. In the latter end of June and in July the worm is most deadly in sunshine; indeed, it is generally during that period deadly only in sunshine; and when the sun *glares* all the water it is most deadly of all. The reason of this, we are of opinion, is that trout cannot see the angler so well when the sun shines on the water as otherwise; and when it causes the streams and pools to glare or shine, the angler may capture them even in shallow water at a few feet from his rod-point, so difficult it would seem is it for trout to see under such waters. When the water is shining thus, the angler, if walking on the river bed or on a level with it cannot see the river bottom; hence it may be assumed that trout may have the same difficulty to contend with when trying to observe objects on the land or in the upper element. Through the medium of the water, refraction will we know soften the brilliancy of the sun's rays for the finny tribes; but as trout have no eyelids, we are of opinion that the rays that reach them from strong sunlight, however much modified by refraction, must to a considerable extent favour the angler's approach to their haunts. We know, however, some good anglers who hold that the reason why trout take worms so freely in midsummer sunshine is, that under the pleasure of basking near the edges and in the shallows of stream and pool, they become somewhat forgetful, and—being like charity children, always ready for "some'at to eat"—readily gobble the angler's bait.

The worm-fisher must cast up-stream, and keep well back from the place in which he expects to make a capture; and to enable him to do this he should have a 14 or 15 feet rod. If he cannot keep out of sight of the trout he tries to take, he may as well go home at once. He should also learn to throw a long line—and that without causing the worm to slip down the hook or break on the tackle-hooks —because in all large waters, and often where banks are awanting in small waters, unless he throw a long line he cannot make his lure reach the trout without being personally seen by them. When a trout is felt, after allowing a second or two to pass, the angler should *strike* down-stream, or as near as he can against the direction in which the trout is thought to be lying. With the *tackle* worm-hooks he should strike the moment he feels a touch, as in fly-fishing. Streams are the principal places in which to fish, but the angler should remember that in June and July the trout are scattered over all the river, and are plentiful in odd corners and side streams where the water is often not more than four or five inches deep; hence no places of such description should be missed by him; indeed, they often yield most sport, as trout mostly all feed at the sides, where worms are always most plentiful. If a wind should happen to be blowing up the valley, the worm-angler reaps some benefit therefrom, as he may then angle in pools as well as streams. The least wind-ripple on a pool partly prevents the trout from noticing the accompaniments of the angler's bait, which so often frighten them from taking; and they often, when the surface is rippled, take the worm as they take fly, the moment it alights on the water. For pool-fishing of this description the angler of course requires to throw a light long line, and to have fine gut in use.

An ordinary bait hook for worm-fishing does very well at the beginning of the season, when the trout are still unjealous of the worms coming to them in such a stiff form; but in July, when rivers are at their smallest, and trout are extremely wary, many of them having been hook-nipped, we prefer using a tackle of three small hooks, upon which we stick the worm in such a way that it can wriggle about in a quite natural style; and we find the liveliness of the worm always makes up for the visibility of the small hooks used, for trout take the worm in this form fully more freely than when bent round a common bait-hook. The tackle form does not answer in Tweed so well as in the smaller streams, because the larger worms generally used in Tweed often, from their liveliness, turn and twist themselves and tackle into a knot, in which shape no trout will have them. The tackle breaks and wastes more worms than the single hook.

The best angling-worms for the Tweed are the *black-headed* worms, the size of which varies much, and the angler may use the size he finds most deadly. The *black-headed* worms are also good for small stream angling, but it is often difficult to procure them small enough—about four inches or so in length. We always use smaller worms for fishing the Tweed than are used by the anglers we are in the habit of meeting on that stream, and they are numerous ; but we have sometimes, though seldom, found worms of a larger size than we use taken when smaller worms were refused. This was generally on days when the weather was changeable. For Teviot and the smaller waters, such as Kale or Leader, we prefer the *marsh-worm*. This worm is often abundant in dampish stackyards, and in old rubbish heaps, and if in a breeding state, has a white *knot* some distance from its head. If not amorously inclined, the white knot is represented by only a whiteish ring. These worms when scoured are beautifully pink, and they are seldom too large for the angler.

Brandling worms require much longer keeping than other worms in order to toughen sufficiently, to allow of easy baiting; and for clear water angling in small rivers, our experience leads us to consider them next to the *marsh* worm as a bait. Anglers who keep a stock of worms should note too, that brandlings are much more easily kept alive than any other kind of worms. Even should the moss in which they may be placed for toughening become mildewed or partly rotten, a slight sprinkling of water over the moss will keep them quite lively. Remembering where they are bred, this is not to be wondered at.

———

It has often been wondered at how trout and other fishes have such a greedy appetite for worms, land animals; and none of our naturalists try to account for it. Knapp, in his delightful and often quoted *Journal of a Naturalist*, even writes as

follows :—" Secured as the worm appears to be by
its residence in the earth from the capture of
creatures inhabiting a different element, yet many
aquatic animals seem well acquainted with it, and
prey on it *as a natural food whenever it falls in
their way.*"

Within the last two or three years we have
made many investigations in the river-beds of the
Tweed and Teviot and other smaller waters, and
from these we have learned how it comes that fishes
have such a relish for worms. We found that many
more worms reside in the river-beds, under water,
than could be found by digging in an equal surface
of earth along the water's edge. We knew many
years ago, as no doubt many anglers also know, that
worms were not uncommon under the pebbles in
river-beds; but not until a comparatively recent
date did we know that they are so very numerous.
We have often found two or three worms below a
single pebble, and we got them from where the
water scarcely covered the stones, to a depth of
twelve or fourteen inches; and where the stones
were imbedded in clayey soil we found at least a
worm for every third or fourth stone turned over.
Where the stones had clay beds the worms too
were larger than where the stones were lying on

sand. They are what are commonly called *water-worms*, but they are constructed like earth worms, and a novice would not know them from these. There are two kinds in the rivers; one very black-headed, dark on the back, reddish on the sides, and flattish : this is the largest of the two, and may be found from two to six inches long. The other is dark-headed, and inclined to yellow, and sometimes green, and *ringed* in the body.

Many anglers and authors think that the worms by which trouts get gorged in a flood are brought into the rivers by flooded drains and the like, whereas they get gorged from their own river-beds; because the floods generally turn over large numbers of pebbles and thereby dislodge the worms in thousands. On examining the worms in a trout's throat or maw, the angler will find that as a rule no other than water-worms are ever lodged there; and after a flood almost all large trout on being captured show numbers of them, half-mashed and otherwise, in their gullets.

These worms too, along with numerous small water-grubs (most of which eventually become trout flies), are what cause ducks to gobble and *plouter* so much about the edges of drains, burns, rivers, and mill-ponds. What else could they capture? Two summers ago, the writer and a friend watched the movements, for a considerable time, of a few ducks in the Jed. The water was so clear that the heads of the ducks were seen in all their movements under the water; and during the time they were watched they were constantly moving aside or turning over the pebbles over which they were swimming. From this it is evident that their food at the water's edge must bear a pretty large portion of water worms.

We have heard it alleged that trout will not take these worms when angled with; but such is not the case, as we have several times used them with success; but we fished with them of necessity, and would rather have had a supply of well-scoured earth worms.

The reason, in our opinion, why trout are so fond of worms in mid-summer is not, as many anglers say, because they are tired of flies, but because they have nothing else almost to feed upon. The grub flies have mostly all left the bottom of the river by midsummer, and the eggs of the earlier flies cannot, we opine, be grown so as to yield sufficient food for trout until the flush of summer is past; so that worms are almost the only abundant dish to be had at such a season. Another

12

thing that may tend to make trout prowl about the edges of rivers, and nose around and under the pebbles in midsummer is, that worms at this season are wriggling under the influence of Cupid, and when paying love visits to each other they all but leave their holes or cells, and thereby expose themselves to the watchful eye and ready mouth of the trout. Worms begin to meet about the end of April in mild weather, and breed all through the summer.

SCRAP.

WATER INSECTS.

DURING the last year or two we have endeavoured to watch the rise and progress of a pretty large family of water or river insects ; and in order to try as far as possible to come to correct conclusions, we on several occasions and in several places collected numerous grubs, and placed them in their native element, with a surrounding of pebbles. And as we always had these enclosures in private waters, where they were never disturbed by anglers or boys, we anticipated being able in a year or two to note the natural history of most of them. This, however, we have not been able to do : indeed we have just learned sufficient to make us remain silent. We find that instead of a year or two, it would require many years' careful observation, in order to note correctly the history of the grubs and flies inhabiting our running waters, for a number of drawbacks come in the way of observation. The water is always running pretty freely over the places where

insects are most abundant; and we found that the
stone enclosures in these places could not be made
sufficiently close to keep in the grubs we lodged in
them : even the putting together a considerable
number of them, alone seemed to make them think
something was wrong; and until their number was
reduced to about the ordinary figure, escape seemed
the only end in view with most of them. Sometimes, too, when we were on the tip-toe of expecta-
tion from noticing changes about to take place in
the vesture of some particular grub, a sudden rising
of the river swept both insects and enclosures away.
Loaches (or beardies) often also thinned our pre-
serves, and in this they were occasionally helped
by small eels. Whenever beardies got within an
enclosure containing only creepers and caddis worms,
in a very short space of time the beardies alone
were left, so rapacious are these small fishes. It is,
besides, a very difficult thing to distinguish one grub
from another of its kind, and whenever very few
were encircled they always disappeared.

The "creeping things," and animalculæ and grubs
fastened, like shell fish, to the river stones, are vastly
numerous, and in the winter season when no surface
food is within reach of the denizens of the deep, an
abundant supply of food is thus always procurable.

And before trout-flies leave the river bottom to sport in the upper element, they are full grown and complete, and we have often taken them thus grown and winged out of their semi-transparent cases, formed of a skin resembling gelatine, even in the late autumn. When we see trout leaping and feeding *en masse* on flies, the "take is on," as anglers term it. and thousands of flies may be seen floating and eddying on the surface, their wings standing erect like tiny sails. The sudden rise of the flies from the bottom to the surface is the cause of the "take," and from this it would appear that from the few minutes they inhale the air before being crushed in the maw of the trout, they acquire a richer flavour than they possess in the water.

It is believed that all trout flies are produced from eggs dropped into the water; and we can speak of one fly we have often seen in the act of dropping eggs—the stonefly. This fly drops its eggs near the edges of streams, not pools. The fly leaves *terra firma*, where it runs among the grass blades that float or overhang the river, and paddles into the stream a few feet, sometimes a yard or two, dropping its small black eggs the while, which by their specific gravity speedily reach the bottom and settle beneath stones. The fly repeats this process of egg-dropping for hours at a time. After every deposit it paddles to the shore, where it rests among the grass or pebbles for a short time, and then renews its labour. We have heard it asserted that a trout will not take a fly in the act of depositing its eggs, but we have witnessed something different; and we have no doubt but any trout will just as readily gobble an egg-dropping fly as a poacher will spear or net a spawning trout or salmon.

BIOGRAPHICAL.

As John Younger was a Borderer, and as his book refers almost solely to angling in border streams, it may not be deemed improper herein to record a few words on two noted border anglers now deceased. We shall begin with

JOCK SMAIL.

Jock Smail, who died about twelve years ago, was a Jedburgh man; and his principal angling streams were the Teviot, Rule, Jed, and Kale. He was for a long term of years looked upon as, and he no doubt was, the most successful angler in the district. His feats with fly on the still pools of the Jed are

yet spoken of; and we have seen him fill a moderate
creel out of one long pool where almost no other
angler would have taken above half-a-dozen trouts;
and at this time he considered himself past his best,
for he was an oldish man. He had a thorough
knowledge of the habitat of all the finny tribes in
the streams he fished; and his feats were performed
with what would now be called very coarse tackle.
He was also the most successful Teviot salmon
angler in his day; and he it was who found out the
minnow to be a bait for salmon. Early in the
present century (about 1805 or '6), he was angling
one day in the Teviot for salmon, in company with
his father—"Auld Rob," also a keen and clever
angler. The old man, after vainly plying his fly
for an hour or two, came to Jock, calling out as he
approached, " c'way, c'way, they're no gaun to take;
let's hame;" but on seeing three or four fish lying
grassed, he immediately˙ ejaculated—"lord! how
gat ye thae, callant?" Jock did not explain; but
Rob, watching his " cast," cried out, " mercy, laddie,
yer flye fa's like a stane, what are ye fishing wi'?"
The minnow was shown, and the twosome kept the
secret for a season or two, during which time they
killed a large number of fish. The fish taken by
the minnow were bull-trouts and salmon kelts, but

in those days kelts were counted salmon. John Smail, like John Younger, was a shoemaker, respectable and respected, and like him he dressed flies, by which he eked out his living. Both father and son fished from boyhood to old age.

JAMES BAILLIE

Was, we do not hesitate to say, the best fly-fisher ever known in the Borders. We have mentioned him in some of our notes to the present work, and some of these were printed before he died, his demise having taken place in November 1861, at the age of forty six. He angled almost solely in the Leader and the Gala, and he seldom tried from spring to autumn any other lure than fly. In the hottest days of June and July, when these waters were at their smallest, and when almost no angler ever thought of trouting with fly, he could, every day, and in a few hours' fishing, kill from 10 to 15 lbs. of trout. For many years before his death he was in feeble health, and he could not stand the fatigue of fishing more than four or five hours a day; and during these years he had to refrain from wading, as wetting his feet would have prostrated him entirely. He fished always up-stream, and his principal flies were "spiders," thinly dressed. He spoke of shop-made spiders as "liker bottle brushes than speeders." His rod (not by choice, but necessity, for he was always poor, and had to live by his angling) was of unpeeled hazel : it was of two pieces, and when tied up it was well balanced and bent with every cast down to the hand. His mode of casting was a firm throw from the elbow ; and he could throw a very long light line, and make the hooks fall on the very spot he wished. He did not like very fine gut, but when he had a choice he always picked the roundest strands. His gut, however, unless some one had presented him with it, was generally coarse ; because he had to purchase it in pennyworth's in country shops, where little choice could be had. We met him on the Leader one April day, and we never saw a coarser casting-line than he was using. The strands had been knotted down and down until we are certain the longest did not exceed six inches ; and with that line, which was of a milky-white colour (for he almost never stained the gut he purchased), he had captured upwards of eight dozen trouts that day. A peculiarity of his angling was that he seldom caught very small trouts : this we noticed many a time when angling alongside of him. He was often in very poor circumstances during the winter season, especially of late years, as he was not

strong enough to shift about for a living, in the way
he did when in health.   He called upon us two
months or so before he died, in miserable health, and
thinly clad, and we had the satisfaction of seeing
him leave with a lighter heart.   He was of gipsy
extraction, we believe, and from anything we know to
the contrary—and we saw a good deal of him during
the later years of his life—he was honest and trust-
worthy.   Let anglers note this: he blamed his
incessant wading in his early years for his early
death.

HOMEWARD ROUTE.

PERHAPS the greatest drudge connected with angling
is after a long and successful day's sport, to have to
walk a number of miles before reaching home, under
the pressure of a heavy basket and an empty stomach,
accompanied sometimes with a burning sun and a
dusty hard road.   We have made this "weary pil-
grimage" so often that in reflective moments, when
that part of a day's sport comes into view, we sometimes break into a perspiration—the very remembrance of it is so overpowering.   We shall narrate,
however, the way we have found it most easy to get
over the ground under such circumstances, hoping

that it may at some time prove beneficial to some poor "unfortunate, weary of breath :"—We use *tacketed* shoes, of a size large enough to admit wading stockings when required; but when we wade without the water-tights, in order to keep the shoes firm and easy on our feet, we put a quantity of soft grass into them. After finishing our sport we take off our shoes, wash them out, and turn them up to drip. We then pull some of the softest grass we can find and put a layer of it into them, put on a pair of dry socks, which are easily carried in the pocket, and then put on the shoes. After this we can generally reach home without getting foot-sore. The basket (and note this, for it is of importance) we raise so high upon our back that it half rests on the shoulders, and we easily keep it in that position by twisting our rod once round the belt in front of us, and letting our arms rest on the rod— one arm on each side of the belt; and the belt can be taken up a few links if found too long for this. The arms have thus a sort of lever power upon the basket, which makes it feel lighter, from the weight being more equally divided, and the *basket shoulder* being relieved from the dead weight.

DESCRIPTIVE LIST

OF ALL THE

SALMON ROD-CASTS IN THE TWEED,

INCLUDING THE NAMES OF PROPRIETORS.

———◆———

WITH very few exceptions, these casts have been corrected by the proprietors themselves; and, barring the changes that floods may have caused since the corrections were made, they will be found correct. From anglers and others well acquainted with the Tweed, in different districts, returns were also kindly sent in, bearing lists both of proprietors and casts, and from these the Editor had thus the whole casts thoroughly checked. Some of the statements did not tally exactly as to the proprietorship of the first or last cast in some fishings, but in cases where two proprietors made a claim, enquiry was made, and the correct name placed against such casts.

The casts herein appear in the order in which they follow each other on the river.

Thanks are herewith offered to the proprietors and friends who so courteously corrected the casts sent them for that purpose.

Salmon are occasionally taken with fly as high up as Biggar Water Foot; but hitherto poaching has been carried on so extensively in these higher waters, that the angler had seldom a chance of hooking a salmon unless immediately after a flood; but the better system of watching put into execution at the commencement of the close-time in 1862 may tend to improve the sport of the rodsman. Beginning about three miles above Peebles the casts come in order as follows:—

The Inch. In the middle of this pool there is a small island.

Barn's Pool.

Brown Knowe Goat.

Long, or *Mid Pool.*

The Wickers.

Eddstone Heuch.

Manor Foot.

The land on the south side of these casts belongs to Barns and the Earl of Wemyss, and the north side, with the exception of a small haugh, also belongs to the Earl of Wemyss.

Upper Poples. Fine spawning stream.

Nether Poples. Fine spawning stream.

Stay Pool, or *Wood Pool.*

Toll Pool. .

Allery Stream.

Stone-Dyke Foot.

Castle-back. One of the finest casts about Peebles.

Dove Cots.   .

Howden. A fine spawning stream.

Little Wood Pool.

Minister's Pool.

  Earl of Wemyss proprietor on both sides.

Cowford Stream, at Peebles Bridge. A fine spawning stream.

The Factory Stream, near Peebles.

The Drain.

Arthur's Putt.

Hay Side. Spawning stream.

Kerfield Pool.

Broad Stream.

Booner Staff.

Nether Staff.

Kerfield on the north side of the two last mentioned.

The Wheel, or *Wire Bridge.* A good spawn bed.

Hunter's Stream. A good spawn bed.

Eshielsback Water. A good spawn bed.

Haystone Burnfoot.

Scotsmill-back

Dog Craig.

Kailzie Throat.

King's Meadows on both sides.

Kailzie Pool.

Castle Pool.

Red Yett, opposite Kailzie.

Maggie's Tail.

Laidlaw's Heuch Cheek.

Kirkbank Boat Pool, Cardrona side.

The Rumbler.

The above on Pirn; and Nether Horsburgh on north side, and Cardrona on south side, down to Traquair Water.

The Dirt Pot, three miles below Peebles, on Nether Horsburgh farm. Strong, rough, deep, rocky cast.

The Cragg, head of Nether Horsburgh nut wood. Fine cast from Cardrona side.

Wood-end Pool. Fine cast over rough stones.

Glenormiston property begins here, north side.

The Girley. A strong rough cast, deep on Cardrona side.

Fawn-burn Pool. Fine spring cast.

TRAQUAIR WATER.

Lord Traquair is proprietor on the south side of all the casts to Kame-knowe-end, and on north side to Leithen foot.

The Whins. A fine gravelly pool; fine spawning at the upper part of it.

The Jawstane.

The last two belong to Glenormiston on north side.

New Water. Beginning with a long ford stream, rough bottomed, a fine gravelly pool below.

Pirn from Leithen foot to Hollylee.

Cowford. A thin stream where fish spawn occasionally; falls into

Traquair Boat Pool. A cast in heavy water —best for spring fishing.

Quair-Foot, opposite Traquair House. Pool, rocky and deep on south side; a good cast when the water is of proper size.

Upper Drown-Pouch, a little below Traquair Bridge. Good for spawning—good for trouting—middling for salmon.

Nether Drown-Pouch. Good salmon cast.

Cadon-bank Pool. Excellent salmon cast, deep and rocky on south side.

Haugh-head Pool. Good cast—upper part spawning stream; the pool deep and rocky on north side.

Mound Pool. Very good for salmon and trout.

Bishop's Point. An excellent new cast.

The Clure. A very fine cast.

Gazeling-Dale — upper and nether casts. The nether cast is the best.

Weaver's Pool—upper and nether casts. Both good casts.

Picklarny. Good for clean salmon.

Three Bold Throats. Three deep gullies—good rough rugged casts — the lowest the best; a fish hooked in the upper leads the fisher a dance to follow it down to the under.

Bold Burnfoot.

Barn Wa's—below Tweeddale Mills. Grand salmon pool.

Ashtree Stream. Not a fly cast. Below the stream is a strong throat, a good fly cast.

Litster, or *Lidster-heuch.* A deep pool on south side.

Caberston Rack, opposite Juniper Bank. Fine spawning stream; pool below a good cast for grilse.

For a good distance below this the water is thin and good for trouting. From this to Hollylee Boat Pool inclusive, the casts on the north side belong to Hollylee.

Bar Pool. A famed pool for salmon and trout; rocky on north side.

13

Kame-knowe-end — mutual. A good cast from the south side.

From this to the head of the river the proprietors are lenient, and anglers generally enjoy their sport without interruption, looking upon the fishing as free.

End of Traquair Water.

ELIBANK WATER—

On the south side down to Nout Sykes inclusive.

Birky Throat, near to foot of Gatehopeknowe. A very fine cast.

Hollylee Boat Pool.

Howegate.

Belongs to Capt. Mitchell of Stow, and all the casts on the north side, down to Gleddie's Wheel inclusive.

Howegate, for about half-a-mile below this, consists of deep heavy water, with three casts at different places on the north side. It is a good salmon hold, and for fly-fishing when the water is full.

Elibank Wood Pool. A deep pool, famous for kelts.

The water divides here, there being a fine island in the middle.

Rough Haugh. Fine strong rapid stream, for salmon and grilse.

Nout Sykes. A spawning stream.

End of Elibank Water.

ASHIESTEEL WATER.

The four following casts belong on the south side to Ashiesteel. On the north side the two first belong to Capt. Mitchell; then Torwoodlee comes in on the north, and goes down on that side to Little Caddon-foot.

Steel Pool. A fine cast both for salmon and trout; rocky bottom, water swift, trouting part of it rough but not deep.

*Gleddie's Wheel.** A fine pool cast at all seasons

Rampiheugh. Salmon cast.

Ashiesteel Boat-hole. Grilse and kelts

End of Ashiesteel Water.

————

The Duke of Buccleuch is proprietor on the south side of the three following casts :—

Peel Boat-hole. A fine cast for late grilse and salmon, lower part best for trouting ; a mutual cast.

Peel Putt. A good cast for grilse and kelts.

Peel Burn-foot. A good cast for grilse and kelts; a mutual cast

* It was in this pool that Sir Walter Scott, Hogg, and some of their friends had such a fine ducking by the breaking up of their boat when leistering salmon, which, as Hogg said, quoting from "Guy Mannering," were "turning up sides like swine."

YAIR WATER.

Pringle of Yair is proprietor of the south side down to Russell's Rock, half-a-mile below Yair Bridge; but on the portion below the bridge the Fairnielee property has a right of fishing mutually with Yair.

Craig Stream.   Good for a clean salmon.

Craig-on Gullets.   Counted one of the best casts in the district; rocky on north side.

Moss Pool.   Good pool cast.

Little Caddon-foot.   Upper half on Torwoodlee; under half belongs to Major Scott, who has also the next cast.

End of Torwoodlee Water—north side.

Caddon Foot.   This is a first-rate salmon cast.

Gled Heugh.   A good cast for kelts.

The following casts, down to Ettrick foot, on the north side, belong to Fairnielee :—

Blakie's Haugh.   A very poor cast.

Needpath.   Famous cast at any season.

Boglehouse Stream.   A middling cast.

Yair Boat Pool.   Famous for kelts, and in heavy water in Autumn.

Elm Wheel.   Fine for clean fish.

Yair Rocks, or *Trows.*   Clean fish in summer or early autumn in small waters.

Gipsy Bog.   For a clean grilse.

Brander. Easy for kelts.

Burnet's Cairn. For kelts.

Raelee's House-back. Fair water for grilse and kelts.

Russell's Rock. For kelts and "late" big fish. A mutual cast.

End of Yair Water.

SUNDERLANDHALL WATER.

Howden Rack, or *Pot Stream.* A famous spawning bed, and a good late spring cast.

Arras's Putt. Fine for a clean fish; half a mile of trouting water down to the Tweed Bridge.

Sunderlandhall Boat Pool. Fine trouting pool.

Black Strand. Spawning bed.

Tweed Bridge, at Ettrick Foot.* Spawning-stream, and a fair cast.

End of Sunderlandhall and Haining water—south and north sides.

BOLDSIDE WATER,
Belonging to Major Scott of Gala (both sides).

Meeting Pool—junction of Ettrick and Tweed. Good cast.

* Salmon enter the Ettrick freely, and rod-fishing is sometimes very good in it; but, with the exception of about a mile-and-a-half of water at Selkirk, the only parts of the river worth the salmon angler's attention are preserved.

Rink Stream.   Excellent for clean fish.

Hedging-end Pool.   Principally a kelt pool, or salmon at backend.

Garden Back Stream.

Garden Back Pool.   Salmon and grilse, excellent cast.

Boldside Wheel.   Fine long rocky pool, good for any kind of fish.

Glen Mein.   Good for salmon and spring fish, long and deep.

Hart-pool.   A famous salmon cast; a spawning stream above.

Hind's-house Pool.   Easy pool for a kelt.

Foghouse.   Easy pool.

Dead Water Heugh.   Easy water for kelts.

Gala Foot.   A deep excellent cast, but exceedingly changeable from the floodings of the Gala.

End of Boldside Water.

LORD SOMERVILLE'S WATER.

Carey Wheel.   A good salmon cast amongst rough rugged rocks.

Railway Bridge Pool.   A small cast.

Glass-Wheel Pot—below the Railway bridge.   A deep whirl, rocky on north side.

Knares.   Fine cast, half pool, half stream.

Bridge-end Pool. Deep pool, the stream falling into it; a good cast as far as the run goes into the pool below Langlee, and opposite the hamlet of Bridge-end.

Quarry Stream. A rapid good cast.

King's Well Lees, or *Big Brae.* An excellent stream-cast, at the foot of Elwand, or Allan water.

Meg's Pool—a stream forming a pool below. A good cast opposite the fisherman's house.

Carre's Shot. A middling cast below Melrose Stone Bridge.

The Whorles, or *Hallow Weel*—a stream falling into a deep pool. A good cast for salmon and grilse.

Boatshiel. A small cast, but good.

Elm Weel. A stream falling into a fine deep pool cast.

Auld Brig. A cast in full water, opposite Gattonside House Lodge.

Sauter's Ford Stream. A cast in any water, nearly opposite St. Helen's House.

Cauld Pool. A fine hold for fish all the year, and good fishing from a boat. In spring contains great abundance of kelts.

Cauld-back. A cast, but often altering.

The Battery. A capital stream—part rocky.

Cowey's Hole. Mutual. A first-rate stream.

The under part of Cowey's Hole is on Drygrange Water.

End of Lord Somerville's Water.

DRYGRANGE WATER.
Thomas Tod of Drygrange, proprietor.

Eddy Stream. Rapid, subject to alterations by floods.

Miller's Turn. Good cast.

Buller's. Rugged gully, ending in a pool-cast.

Lang Cairn. Good spring cast.

Fly-bridge Pool. Capital cast in a full water.

End of Drygrange Water.

OLD MELROSE WATER.
George K. E. Fairholme, proprietor of south side; John Meikleham of Gladswood, proprietor of north side down to Cromwell, half inclusive; then Miss Haig, Bemersyde, on north side, to end of Old Melrose Water.

Leader-foot Pool. Long cast, for spring and autumn.

Rampiheugh. Good, long, strong, stream cast.

Long-cairn. Stream, deep and very good.

The Coburns. Good stream cast.

Paddock-heads. Good, soft stream cast.

Cromwell. A splendid pool-cast—fine hold for fish.

Gateheugh Streams, in five or six breaks. All excellent casts.

Hally-Wheel Throat. Never "out of a tenant." Only the *throat* of this cast belongs to Old Melrose.

End of Old Melrose Water.

BEMERSYDE WATER.

Miss Haig proprietor on both sides.

Middle-streak Hole. Pool and stream.

The Cradles. Long, half-stream, half-pool, rocky bottom.

Sangster's Point. Good on north side occasionally.

Between the above cast and the following one there are two good casts in spring and autumn, when the water is fuller.

Jock-sure, or the *West Wood.*

Buss aboon Traquair. Pool on south side for spring fishing.

End of Bemersyde Water.

DRYBURGH WATER.

This water belongs to Captain Riddell.

Battery. Strong good stream.

Toad-holes. Fine cast, stream and pool; including the two following casts.

The Throat.

Mungie.

Beehill. Excellent long cast.

Wire-bridge Pool. A fair cast.

Dryburgh Boathole. Capital cast, but rather hurt by the ferry-boat.

Caul-Pool. A good rocky cast, opposite Major Riddell's house.

Tommy Tulloch's Throw; below Dryburgh cauld-dyke.

Howden Burn-foot. A strong throat, and good cast for summer.

Harecrag.* Very good for all seasons.

Burn-foot. Stream and pool; a good throw for all seasons.

Brockie's Hole. Good for all seasons.

Gullet. A sure summer cast at the cairn point.

Birkieheugh. A cast of medium character; fair for spring fish.

Back o' the Stenhouse. A first-rate cast for kelts.

Lang Stream. Good all the year—salmon and grilse.

End of Dryburgh Water.

MERTOUN WATER.

Lord Polwarth, proprietor.

West Indies. For spring fishing.

The Caul Pool. A fine cast in all seasons—quite a hold for fish.

The Caul Dyke-back. A good stream.

Broom-ends. Spring cast.

Back-brae. Stream—a capital cast.

---

* From the overhanging Gray-crag, the author once counted in this cast forty-two salmon, all lying on the principal bottom rock, and held there for weeks in consequence of the lowness of the water.

Strong Stream, or *Jock A.-B.* Summer cast.

Kipperha' Stream. A fair summer cast.

The Pot. Grand, deep, rocky cast.

Gibson's Hole. A very good spring cast.

The following casts, down to the middle of The Webbs, belong on the south side to Sir Henry Fairfax.

Benrig Caul-stream. A summer cast, soft near the foot—kelts and salmon.

Haugh Side. South side for spring fishing.

Kirk-back. ˙Stream and pool—good.

Three Breaks. For summer salmon or grilse.

Cast above the Webbs. Good salmon stream.

The Webbs. A fine deep cast—excellent in all seasons.

Crago'er. A splendid cast, and a hold for fish in all seasons.

Stile-well. Stream—good—just above Mertoun house.

Stile-foot. Famous pool below.

House Stream. Good.

Willow Bush. Fine spring pool.

Caller Haugh Fine stream and pool.

Tower Stream (Littledean Tower.) Good.

End of Mertoun Water.

RUTHERFORD WATER.

Sir Edmond Antrobus, proprietor.

This, as a whole, is most excellent fishing water.

Corseheugh.   A fine pool—mutual between Mertoun and Rutherford.

Lang-stream.

Dub.   Good in spring.

Stream between the Caulds.

Mill Stream.

Lover's Loup.   Stream.

Corbie.   Stream.

Clippers.   Stream.

End of Rutherford Water.

MAKERSTOUN WATER.

Lady Makdougall Brisbane, proprietor.

Willie's Bank.   Spring cast for kelts and grilse.

Hirple Nellie.*   Good for kelts and trout.

Orchard Head.   Fine cast for salmon and kelts.

Dark Shore.   Fine cast for salmon and kelts.

North and South Clippers.   Good summer casts for clean salmon.

Laird's Cast.   For salmon and kelts.

Elshie Stream.   Fair cast for salmon and kelts.

Head of Blakeman.   For salmon and kelts.

* An English sporting literateur lately translated the above name into "Help our Nelly." How he will relish his *Dunbar !*—[Edr.]

Red Stane. Fine rising cast for salmon and grilse.

Side Strake. For salmon.

Doors. For salmon.

Nethern Heads. For salmon.

Runners. A summer cast for salmon.

Kill Mouth. For salmon and kelts.

End of Makerstoun Water.

FLOORS WATER.
Belongs to His Grace the Duke of Roxburghe.

[We do not consider it necessary to give a descriptive list of the individual casts in Floors Water, as it is always kept in the hands of the proprietor. The Duke of Roxburghe is one of the keenest and best salmon anglers on the Tweed, and he owns as fine a stretch of "quiet waters and unquiet waters" as the Tweed can boast of.—EDR.]

The Slates.

Black Stone.

Weetles.

Upper and Lower Huddles.

Shot.

Cauld-slap.

Dyke-end.

New Stream.

Hedge-end.

Shirk Stream.

Lang-rocks, or *Dam Foot.*

Skelly Rock.

Planting-end.

Coach Wynd.

Innes' Cast.

Income.

Garden Wall, or *Cobble Hole.*

Putt.

Back Bullers.

Teviot Foot, or *The Junction.*

The Teviot, after a flood, often yields very good sport, and on application to Mr Darling of Broomlands, or to Mr Darling, Banker, Kelso, a free ticket may be obtained, stating that the bearer "has the Duke of Roxburghe's permission to fish for salmon on the north side of the river Teviot, from Ormiston March to Maxwellheugh Mill Cauld"—a stretch of nearly four miles of the best fishing-water in the river.—EDR.]

Cradles.

*Maxwheel.**

End of Floors Water.

———

SPROUSTON WATER.

The south side belongs to the Duke of Roxburghe; the north, from Mill-stream to Eden Water-foot, both inclusive, to John Waldie of Hendersyde.

The water is held in lease by one of the Tweedside Kersses, and from him anglers can procure fishing on reasonable terms; and with such water and such fishermen no fair angler can miss a salmon if he will bite at all. The Sprouston water, as a whole, is first-rate. The Dub is the finest cast in the Tweed, and, from its dimensions and resources as a salmon-hold, yields a day's sport to more than one angler.

---

* The Duke of Roxburghe, a few years ago, killed 6 salmon and 20 grilse in one day in Maxwheel.

Hempseed Ford. Excellent stream.

General's Bank. Stream at top, and pool below.

Grain. Rapid stream—excellent.

Mill Stream. Long and good; rapid at top.

Mill Pot. A spring and fall cast.

Butterwash. Good grilse cast.

Bushes. Half stream and pool—fine rocky cast.

Rock. Good, particularly in low water.

Prison. Very good and deep.

Dub. The best cast yet named; long, broad, and deep, admits boats all over.

Caul-back. Short stream, good and sure.

Mill-end. Good for big water.

Faulds. Long cast, rather a pool.

Eden Water-foot. A fine spring cast, half streamy, rippling, broken water.

Birgham Dub. Large, first-rate cast—south side.

Burn Stream. Good rough cast—south·side.

End of Sprouston Water.

CARHAM WATER.

Earl of Home proprietor of north side, and J. H. Hinde, Esq., of the south side as far down as the Under Cairn Neb, from which to the end of Carham Water, Richard Hodgson of Carham is proprietor.

The casts in Carham Water, as a whole, are mostly rocky, and all are good.

Birgham Dub, north side. Grand cast.

Wheel Stream, north side.   Rough broken water —very good.

Carham Wheel.   Good, especially when the water is low.

Ship-end.   Middling—good trouting. •

Long ship-end—also called the *Prison.*

Flummy, and *Land Cast.*   Good.

Kirk-end.   Very good.

Dritton.   Good.

Glidders.

Bluidy Breeks.

Under Cairn Neb.   Capital cast.

Cauldron Pool.

Head of the Three Stanes.   Fine cast.

Three Stanes.   Fine cast.

Pikey.   First-rate cast.

Three Brethren.   Good.

Nether Stream.   Good.

The Hole.   Good.

The Hole Stream.   Good.

The Neb.   Good in full water.

Craw Stane.   Good.

Merk Skelly Head.   Good.

Bell Stane.   One of the best casts in Carham.

Segg Bush   Middling cast.

White Eddie.   Good.

Whin Bush Skelly. Middling.

Shaws Mere. Good.

Knowe Head. Good.

> End of Carham Water.

LADYKIRK WATER.

The Snipe. Rod cast.

> Lord Ossulton, proprietor.

Lord Home is proprietor of the four following casts.

Wark Dub. Rod cast.

Anna Side. Rod cast.

Cuddie's Hole. Good cast.

Black-mark. Middling cast.

> Sir John Marjoribanks is proprietor of the four
> following casts.

Temple Pool.

Learmouth Haugh.

Battery Wall.

Deddo River-mouth.

> End of Ladykirk Water.

COLLINGWOOD'S WATER.
Three miles of water below Deddo Burn-mouth.

Deddo Mouth. Excellent spring cast.

Trout Hole. Excellent spring cast.

White Stone. Excellent spring cast.

14

Rabbit Nest.   Spring cast—shallow.
Monument Marjoribanks.   Coldstream cast.
Long Cairn.   Good cast, streamy and heavy.
Craw Hole.   Good cast.
Crook Bull.   Good cast.
Rough Stones.   Good cast.
> End of Collingwood's Water.

SIR JOHN MARJORIBANKS' WATER.

Hell's Hole.   Still, rocky bottom.
Temple.   Still, rocky bottom.
Cobble.   Still, rocky bottom.
Cauld Slap.   Ready cast.
Bulwark.   Good cast.
Back o' the Wa'.   Fine cast.
Dead Eye.   Good rocky cast.
Cornhill Stream.   Rough bottom.
> End of Sir John Marjoribanks' Water.

CORNHILL WATER.

East Side of Lees' Haugh.
Boat Hole—ferry before the bridge.
The Craw.   Long-net and rod cast.
English Water.   Rod and net.
Lennel Haugh.

Lord Haddington proprietor on the north side of this and Great Haugh Water.

The Great Haugh Water ; fished by Robert Swan.

Oxendean Burn, down to Tillmouth.

Wellington Cairn. Good cast.

Cauld Slap Chapel Stream. Good cast.

Twizel Boathouse.

Chapel Stream, with part of the Till. Excellent down to Tillmouth.

End of Cornhill Water.

Putt Point, tail of the Chapel stream.

Scarsheugh Rock.

White Cat Rock. Deep and rocky.

Goat's-heugh. Nearly half a mile long—streamy and deep.

Dreeper. Good cast.

Sir Francis Blake and others proprietors of above cast.

Damford. Nearly half a mile long—streamy and deep.

David Robertson, Esq., proprietor of above cast.

Bendibus. Grand long-net shot.

David Robertson, Esq., and others, proprietors of above cast.

Glittery Heuch. From Norham Boathouse to Newbigging Burn, very fine cast.

Mark Young proprietor of above cast.

Westford. Good rod-fishing.

David Robertson, Esq., proprietor of above cast.

Pedwell.   Good rod-fishing.

William Mather, Esq., proprietor of above cast.

Blunt.   Deep good cast.

David Robertson, Esq., proprietor of above cast.

Greenhill.   Good ; about half-a-mile long.

William Mather, Esq. and others, proprietors of above cast.

Hallywell.   Good cast.

David Robertson, Esq., proprietor of above cast.

Callerheugh.   Good cast.

Sir Francis Blake proprietor of above cast.

Wilford.   Good cast.

D. Macbeth and others proprietors of above cast.

Watham Water.   Upwards of a mile in length
The following are the principal casts* :—

Squire.

Boathole, or *Gillies' Rock.*

Geese.

Thompson's Rocks.

Pack About.

Nose End.

Sir Francis Blake proprietor of the above.

Hornwell.   Good cast.

Scotch New Water.   Good cast.

Mr. M'Briar proprietor of the above two casts.

---

* These are all good casts, but the fishing is best when full tides
have not been flowing—the lower the tides the greater the sport with
the rod.

Start. Good cast.

Trustees of Lord Crewe, and Mrs. Shuttleworth, proprietors of above cast.

Finchey, includes two good casts—the *Willow Tree* and the *Cloven Stone.*

David Milne Home proprietor of above cast.

South Bells. Excellent cast at the "Throat."

Low Bells. Excellent for grilse in summer.

Berwick Shipping Company and others proprietors of the above two casts.

END OF SALMON CASTS.

TRIBUTARIES OF THE TWEED,

FOR TROUT ANGLERS.

BY THE EDITOR.

———◆———

The Tweed is a fine trouting river from head to foot, and it is nearly 100 miles in length. Though a longer walk has often to be made from stream to stream than may be required on smaller rivers, the angler has generally the consolation of seeing in the long wide-spreading streams of the Tweed a few hours' respite from pedestrianism. Trout too are plentiful and large; and on none of the tributaries are the appellatives descriptive of large trout so frequently brought into play as on the Tweed. What would Mr. Briggs or his Cockney friends make of terms like these:—*wauper, skelper, bummer, whauker, pinner, yerker, whupper,* and the juvenile exclamation—*aigh! sic a ane!* And relative to large trout, these are terms in common use on the "canny" side of the Tweed.

Tweed is free to trout anglers from its head down to the Pavilion property near Galashiels. From Pavilion to Kelso "notice to trespassers" is the rule, and the exceptions, we are sorry to say, are few and painfully *far* between. On the Pavilion water, we believe, anglers are now seldom, if at all, stopped, more especially about Melrose; but from Leader-foot to Kelso, about eleven miles, there are not more than two places open, and these small. From Kelso to Carham, six miles, trouting is unrestricted. Carham (about a mile) is preserved, but from Wark to Tweedmouth the river is free.

Beginning at the upper part of the Tweed, the first noteworthy stream—though there are many very good burns—is

The TALA—a small water. Fishing good. Angling free.

BIGGAR—a small water. Fishing middling; trout good. The Tweed itself between Biggar Water foot and the Lyne yields very good sport. Angling free.

LYNE, enters the Tweed three miles or so above Peebles. The angling is good, and trout pretty numerous. A mile or two from its mouth the Lyne is joined by the Tarth, which also yields good sport; and all ordinary lures may be used in both streams. Angling free.

MANOR, enters Tweed from the south two miles above Peebles, and is a first-rate trout stream. Angling free.

EDDLESTONE, at Peebles. Fishing not good unless after a flood; the upper part of the water the best. Angling free.

QUAIR, at Innerleithen. Yields good sport to the troutsman, but the trout are small. Some very good burns enter it, the best being Glengaber and Kirkburn. Preserved in neighbourhood of GLEN.

LEITHEN, at Innerleithen, affords very good sport, trout being plentiful; and some good burns enter it, Glentress burn being nearly as good as the Leithen itself. The Leithen is preserved from about four miles above Innerleithen to its source.

CADDON—a burn. Fair fishing after a flood. Angling free.

ETTRICK—a large stream. Angling very good; many good burns about upper sources. The Ettrick is preserved for two or three miles from Yarrow foot upwards.

YARROW, also a large stream, falls into Ettrick two-and-a-half miles above Selkirk; it is preserved for a few miles at the foot. Fishing very good; trouts plentiful, some of them large; many first-rate burns at head.

GALA, although very much fished by anglers from Edinburgh, is first-rate for fly, worm, or minnow-fishing; trouts generally plentiful and good; and some good tributaries join it. Many excellent burns about its source. Angling free.

ELLWAND, or ALLAN—a burn—falls into Tweed two miles below Galashiels. Angling poor, but a fair basket is sometimes made in it after a flood. Angling free.

LEADER, at Earlston; perhaps the best angling stream falling into the Tweed. All the ordinary flies and baits may be fished with successfully; trout a good size and plentiful; many first-rate burns at head of the Leader—three-and-a-half miles at foot preserved, also about a mile at Lauder. The Editor has killed 24 lbs. of trout in the Leader in a day. This was in midsummer when the water was small and clear. BOON water falls into Leader three miles below Lauder. Fishing good, and free.

TEVIOT. Enters the Tweed at Kelso, and is a splendid fishing stream, 35 miles long. Above Hawick the fishing is good, but for a few miles below that town it is rendered useless by the waste dye stuffs from the mills. Where the refuse no longer affects the water it again becomes a good angling stream. Opposite Jedburgh or Lanton the fishing

is best after a flood, and that with fly or minnow;
but when small and clear it is not good for worm-
fishing in this district.   From below Nisbet until it
joins the Tweed, however, it is all that could be desired by an angler—streams plentiful and good—
trouts ditto.   About Ormiston it is preserved, and
also opposite Mounteviot, near Jedburgh, and for
about a mile at Chesters, opposite Lanton.

TRIBUTARIES OF THE TEVIOT.

ALL OF WHICH ARE FREE.

ALLAN—a large burn which comes in four miles
above Hawick.   Fishing middling.

BORTHWICK, two miles above Hawick.   Fishing
fair.

SLITRIG—enters at Hawick.   Lots of trout, and
good fishing, but often spoiled by netters.

RULE—enters four miles above Jedburgh.   Trout
very plentiful but small on lower portion; not so
plentiful, but of heavier dimensions in upper portion.
Fishing easy.   It divides into fine trouting burns
near its head.   The Editor has killed upwards of
twelve dozen in the Rule in a day.   This was on
the lower portion of the river.

ALE—Younger's " native valley"—a small but

pretty long stream, something like the Eden. The angling, as a whole, is very good, and the trout of a good size. It falls into the Teviot below Ancrum.

JED, at Jedburgh. Best trouting after a flood; trout not very plentiful, but good. Easiest angling six or eight miles up, and burns good.

OXNAM—enters three miles below Jedburgh. Fishing pretty good after a flood.

KALE—enters five miles above Kelso, and is the last tributary of the Teviot—a first-rate stream; many good burns at head. Fished a good deal by Jedburgh and Kelso anglers. Trout always plentiful.

The tributaries of the Teviot average 15 miles in length.

EDEN—enters Tweed about three miles below Kelso. It is a very good fishing water, but is mostly preserved.

LEET, at Coldstream. Fair as an angling stream in the spring and early summer—trouts large; most of the water preserved: a very sluggish river.

TILL—below Coldstream. Trouts large, but wary and difficult to take; water deep and sluggish, and preserved here and there. An " early " river. The GLEN falls into it. Fishing in the Glen excellent, but part of it preserved.

Bowmont, a few miles from the Till, is joined by Colledge, and the united rivers from thence to Till are named Glen. Bowmont is an excellent trouting stream from head to foot, and it is a pretty long river. The burns falling into it a few miles above Yetholm are most of them abounding in trout. The only day the Editor ever angled above Yetholm in Bowmont water and some of the burns, he killed upwards of 13 dozen smallish trout, in clear water. Whitling are often taken with the rod in the Bowmont. Angling free.

Whitadder—a long excellent trouting-stream, one of the best; enters Tweed a few miles above Berwick. Some of the burns at its head rise within a few miles of the burns that feed the upper part of the Leader; and we question if two as good trouting rivers, taking them from source to source, enter the Tweed. The Whitadder is fed by a number of fishable burns. Angling free.

Blackadder falls into Whitadder. It is in nature something like Till, sluggish, and trouts large. In the vicinity of Greenlaw fishing good. Preserved for some miles at its mouth.

THE END.

www.ingramcontent.com/pod-product-compliance
Lightning Source LLC
Chambersburg PA
CBHW030102030726
47498CB00007B/2224